Elder Abuse

DATE DUE

		MAR 0 6 2001
	MAR 1 8 2002	
MAR 1 8 2003		
	MAR 2 0 2003	
	JUL 1 3 2010	

D1221779

FORTHCOMING TITLES

Research Methods for Therapists
Avril Drummond

Stroke: Recovery and Rehabilitation
Polly Laidler

Caring for the Neurologically Damaged Adult
Ruth Nieuwenhuis

HIV and AIDS Care
S. Singh and L. Cusack

Speech and Language Disorders in Children
Dilys A. Treharne

Spinal Cord Rehabilitation
Karen Whalley-Hammell

THERAPY IN PRACTICE SERIES

Edited by Jo Campling

This series of books is aimed at 'therapists' concerned with rehabilitation in a very broad sense. The intended audience particularly includes occupational therapists, physiotherapists and speech therapists, but many titles will also be of interest to nurses, psychologists, medical staff, social workers, teachers or volunteer workers. Some volumes are interdisciplinary, others are aimed at one particular profession. All titles will be comprehensive but concise, and practical but with due reference to relevant theory and evidence. They are not research monographs but focus on professional practice, and will be of value to both students and qualified personnel.

Elder Abuse

Concepts, theories and interventions

Gerald Bennett

Consultant Geriatrician
Royal London Hospital

and

Paul Kingston

Lecturer in Nursing
North Staffordshire College of Nursing and Midwifery

CHAPMAN & HALL

London · Glasgow · New York · Tokyo · Melbourne · Madras

Published by Chapman & Hall, 2–6 Boundary Row, London SE1 8HN

Chapman & Hall, 2–6 Boundary Row, London SE1 8HN, UK

Blackie Academic & Professional, Wester Cleddens Road, Bishopbriggs, Glasgow G64 2NZ, UK

Chapman & Hall Inc., 29 West 35th Street, New York NY10001, USA

Chapman & Hall Japan, Thomson Publishing Japan, Hirakawacho Nemoto Building, 6F, 1-7-11 Hirakawa-cho, Chiyoda-ku, Tokyo 102, Japan

Chapman & Hall Australia, Thomas Nelson Australia, 102 Dodds Street, South Melbourne, Victoria 3205, Australia

Chapman & Hall India, R. Seshadri, 32 Second Main Road, CIT East, Madras 600 035, India

Distributed in the USA and Canada by Singular Publishing Group Inc., 4284 41st Street, San Diego, California 92105

First edition 1993

© 1993 Gerald Bennett and Paul Kingston

Typeset in 10/12 pt Palatino by Best-set Typesetter Ltd, Hong Kong
Printed in Great Britain at the University Press, Cambridge

ISBN 0 412 45310 X   1 56593 038 X (USA)

A catalogue record for this book is available from the British Library

Library of Congress Cataloging-in-Publication data available

Contents

Foreword

A book which summarizes what is known about elder abuse has been needed for a long time in this country. A major problem has been the absence of both interest in the subject and research. At long last interest, by academics, practitioners and the media, has stirred. Unfortunately comparisons have too rapidly been made with child abuse.

This book by two of the leading professionals concerned with abuse in the United Kingdom sets out to remedy the gaps in knowledge. In so doing they show how dangerous it is to draw parallels with child abuse and they plead for more theoretical and practical research on the subject. The comparisons which they draw with the United States, where research is more highly developed, are striking.

One of the values of this book is that it starts from first principles and defines what is meant by elder abuse. Starting from what was known as 'granny battering' they show how both definitions and concepts have moved forward. Following the early concentration on physical abuse it is now known that many other kinds are just as pernicious. They include financial, emotional, sexual, psychological abuse and neglect. A particularly useful part of the book shows how research is moving from a study of the abused to that of the abuser. In the course of this the authors destroy some myths such as, for example, that abuse is largely a result of caregiver stress. As the authors say 'The initial stereotyped plot with the victim depicted as female and "old" with physical and mental disabilities being abused by a caring but overburdened daughter has had to undergo rewriting'. The chapter on prevention also destroys some myths such as that professional service providers are trained to assess and treat sexual abuse or that families receiving mental health or social work and other services cannot hide sexual abuse from the professional.

There are many practical parts of the book which will appeal to practitioners. For example the sections on legal issues and the examples from Tower Hamlets bring home the topicality of the subject. For potential researchers the chapter on research is salutary in underlining the problems involved, especially those of ethics and confidentiality.

This well-written book, refreshingly free from jargon, will be welcomed by all who are concerned about the important topic of elderly abuse. Particularly to be commended is the multidisciplinary approach.

Anthea Tinker
Director of the Age Concern, Institute of Gerontology
and Professor of Social Gerontology, King's College, London

Acknowledgements

We are grateful to the numerous authors and their publishers who have given us permission to reproduce some of their work. Many US experts have made us extremely welcome on both study tours and at conferences and we have valued their support and advice. We would particularly like to thank Rosalie Wolf, Karl Pillemer, Jordan Kosberg, Toshio Tatara, Tanya Fusco-Johnson and Terry Fulmer.

I am very grateful to Jim Ogg for his kind permission to reproduce work extensively from his Master's thesis.

In addition we would also like to thank The Department of Health, The British Geriatrics Society, the *Nursing Times*, and *Geriatric Medicine* for their financial support to enable the US study tours to take place.

Finally we have some special thanks. Paul to his wife Ang and daughters Zoe and Lenna for their tolerance of his absence over many weekends. Gerry to his friends Keith, Stephen, Peter, Neil, Mark, Andy, Roger and Kathy, but especially to Hywel and Tim for their love and support.

Introduction

The modern phenomenon of elder abuse was 'discovered' in the UK but the initial momentum was lost and it was left to the Americans to invest time and resources into this extremely important topic. A new momentum is building, however, and abuse of elderly people is destined to become one of the sociomedical topics of the 1990s. We are about to embark on the difficult voyage through the rough waters of definitions, its context in the family violence debate, the worries of the carers lobbies and many other storms. This book relies heavily on data from the US and we offer no apologies. Practitioners there have had a decade of taking this problem seriously and responded with research data, legal reforms and a national information network. It is easy to criticize from over the water; it is a sad reflection that this book contains so few UK references.

This book aims to take both the novice and the hardened professional through what is becoming an increasingly complex arena. It covers the historical background with definitions and theories and then looks at what is currently known about elderly people who are abused and the people that abuse them. We give some insights into the difficult areas of recognition of abuse and its assessment and illustrate possible intervention models. The legal issues on both sides of the Atlantic are discussed and we look to the future with ways in which co-operation between Health and Social Services can help. Many experts feel that prevention strategies are the most important area for future development and various models are given.

The text is meant to be both informative and provocative. We hope that readers will be motivated to pursue the topic locally, reinforcing the need for training, education and research. There is an obvious need for a multidisciplinary group to co-ordinate the various issues involved via a national society and we hope this knowledge base will get formed. A meeting to consider this resulted in a mission statement that encompasses the aims of this book:

To prevent elder abuse by promoting changes in policy and practice through raising awareness, education, research and the dissemination of information.

Gerald Bennett
Paul Kingston

1

Historical background: definitions and theories

HISTORICAL BACKGROUND

Elder abuse and neglect is the latest discovery in the field of familial violence. Nevertheless its importance as one of the major sociological issues of the 1990s will become quickly and uniquely apparent, as did the social problems of child abuse and spouse abuse in the preceding two decades. The two major developments that will exacerbate the already complex phenomenon of elder abuse and neglect are firstly the implications of the changing demography and secondly the policy implications of community care, *Caring for People: Community Care in the Next Decade and Beyond* [1]. Clearly the demographic changes from 1991 through to 2025 will demand greater resources within the community setting. Office of Population, Censuses and Surveys projections suggest an increase from 6.9 million to 8.5 million within the 65–79-year age range and an increase from 2.2 million to 2.9 million for the over-80-year-old range.

It is also important to consider that this population includes increasing numbers of elderly people from differing ethnic backgrounds [2]. Although we do not have any British research to suggest that abuse or neglect is prevalent among differing ethnic groups it may be important to consider the American findings. The American research suggests that elder abuse and neglect does not respect ethnic origin or socioeconomic class. It is possible that British research will replicate these findings. These demographic changes combined with the practical implications of community care changes:

> Community care means providing the services and support which people who are affected by problems of ageing, mental

> illness, mental handicap or physical or sensory disability
> need to be able to live as independently as possible in their
> own homes, or in homely settings in the community. [1]

would suggest increased levels of elder abuse and neglect may
be expected. However, the concept of elder abuse and neglect
as a social problem continues to remain illusive in spite of more
than 15 years of anecdotal articles written by various health
care professionals.

Commentators have suggested that the 1960s was the period
during which child abuse was discovered and the 1970s spouse
abuse (the former by the medical profession and the latter
by the feminist movement). The concept of elder abuse and
neglect as a separate form of familial mistreatment has not yet
gained acceptance as a social problem in Britain. However, it
has been claimed in America [3] that the 1980s would be the
decade when elder abuse and neglect would be discovered. To
a large extent this has been experienced both in America and
Canada [4], though the discovery of elder abuse and neglect in
Britain remains in a formative stage. Ironically the first article
to be traced in English language literature of recent origin
(there are numerous anthropological references to ill-treatment
of elders often to the point of matricide and patricide [5]
was British, namely Baker's 1975 article 'Granny battering' [6].
Baker's article, in retrospect although seen as the formative
work on elder abuse and neglect, was a false lead along the
path to understanding the phenomenon. The term 'granny'
clearly stereotypes elder abuse and neglect as a single-sex
problem and the inference is that only 'grannies' are abused
and neglected. At this point in time the question of abuse and
neglect to 'grandads' was not considered an issue. Beyond
the gender issue there is the stereotyping of a 'granny' as an
elderly white-haired old lady sitting in a rocking chair reading
nursery rhymes to her grandchildren. This stereotype had the
word 'battering' added to it:

> To strike with repeated blows so as to bruise or shatter, to
> subject to crushing or persistent attack or to beat out of
> shape. [7]

The word battering was already in common usage within
the spouse abuse movement with the term 'wife battering' and

this may account for its use at that time. This terminology suggesting only severe physical abuse confused rather than clarified what was conceived as elder abuse and neglect. Beyond this retrospective criticism Baker makes the point that there is evidence of abuse and ill-treatment and more importantly that:

> While sometimes covert it can also occur in situations where it is apparently motivated by good intentions and with the approval of both the professions and the community at large. [6]

This is an issue that has both professional and political repercussions; the elderly are marginalized and facilities for them have been historically underresourced. These are issues that will be returned to. Following this seminal article some two years later came, 'Do your elderly patients live in fear of being battered' [8]. The thrust of Burston's article suggests that lack of both medical and nursing specialization in elderly care allied with ageist attitudes to the elderly are to blame for the phenomenon not being recognized as a social problem. This comment is as true 15 years later as it was in 1977. Burston also had the foresight to suggest that the responsibility for recognizing elder abuse and neglect lies squarely with the primary health care team. Within these two articles differing terminology continued to emerge in the main text including ill-treatment and rejection, and Burston acknowledges this discrepancy by suggesting:

> Granny battering is an emotive phrase, but perhaps it makes people stop and think. [8]

In an international perspective these two articles helped to prompt the Americans to consider the issue of elder abuse and neglect. However, it was not only the medical profession that became involved, the academic fraternity started to consider the issue [9–11]. Within a year the Americans had established a research background to the phenomenon. Within a further year the topic was on the political agenda with United States Congress House Select Committee hearings [12].

Meanwhile the second phase of British articles began to emerge, with Edwards claiming that granny battering is a problem that doctors are failing to detect [13]. Traynor and Hasnip, however, in a perceptive article claimed that:

Table 1.1 Development of terminology

Granny battering
Granny bashing
Granny abuse
Old age abuse
Elder abuse
Elder mistreatment
Inadequate care
Mis-care

... there is simply no firm evidence of an increase in intra-familial abuse of the elderly. [14]

They also suggest that 'granny battering' is an emotive phrase serving to obscure rather than clarify the reality, and the terms 'old age abuse' or 'elder abuse' are preferable. The first call for a major research initiative into both the prevalence and nature of the phenomenon is also made. This particular article was unique because it did not follow the claims made by other authors that cases of elder abuse and neglect were increasing. Eastman at last began to examine the conceptual issues surrounding elder abuse and neglect [15]. Social workers were asked about their views of old age abuse and a definitional discussion began to emerge.

Table 1.1 lists the development of terminology.

The Americans by 1984 had published 27 research papers and elder abuse and neglect was also clearly on the political agenda. In an attempt to establish the same political concern in Britain Andrew F. Bennett MP asked the Secretary of State for Social Services in 1982:

Whether he has any plans to institute research into the incidence of non-accidental injury of elderly people by their relatives? ... what information he has as to how many elderly people are at risk of being physically abused by their care-giving relatives? ... what information is available to him as to the causes of abuse of elderly people by their relatives? [16]

A prevalence figure only emerged a decade later in Britain [17], and only the work of Homer and Gilleard [18] has considered the causation of elder abuse and neglect. The reply from Geoffrey Finsberg claimed:

> Little information is available at present, but independent studies suggest that there is a correlation between a high level of dependency in the elderly person and abuse by a supporter. [16]

This apparent British apathy at a political level explains the immense difference in the development of elder abuse and neglect as a legitimate social problem compared with the trend in America. When the American House Select Committee on Aging inquiry indicated that elder abuse and neglect was occurring nationwide and incidence reports increasing, the impact was public and professional consciousness-raising [12]. Andrew Bennett's attempt to raise the same profile of elder abuse and neglect in Britain as a social problem clearly failed.

The momentum after 1984 was slow to build, Eastman's book *Old Age Abuse* was a noticeable exception [19] but in general anecdotal reports appeared only irregularly in British journals. The Americans were quick to build on the earlier research and enacted 'Mandatory reporting laws' in much the same way that child abuse laws had developed. From 1984 onwards British articles continued to draw attention to the phenomenon although the articles were predominantly aimed at practitioners. The research agenda was non-existent and few agencies were prepared to produce or enact policies and procedures. Within the health care setting the Department of Health produced a performance indicator which asked:

> What arrangements obtain when abuse of an elderly patient is identified or suspected? [20]

Research suggests that few District Health Authorities addressed this 'indicator' even though this checklist was designed to evaluate services in conjunction with the numerical performance indicators [21]. This omission would be unthinkable if the performance indicator had related to child abuse. The momentum appeared to increase when in 1988 the British Geriatrics Society held a major conference aimed at establishing elder abuse and neglect as a social problem [22]. At the conference it became clear that doctors, nurses, therapists and social workers were not prepared to see the phenomenon of elder abuse and neglect remain in the dark. Advice to prevent elder abuse and neglect came in a document jointly published in 1990 [23] by a consortium of:

Age Concern
The British Association of Social Workers
The British Geriatrics Society
The Carers National Association
Help the Aged
The Police Federation of England and Wales

The first research in Britain to assess the prevalence of abuse of elderly people by their carers and also the characteristics of both abused and abuser was completed by Homer in 1990. Homer's research analysed a population of some 71 patient–carer pairs and a further 51 carers and 43 of their patients. Interviews were carried out and risk factors identified in the abused group and compared with a non-abused group. Although definitions were based on Pillemer and Finkelhor's prevalence study [24], limited comparisons can be made as this population was not a random sample. Nevertheless it is useful to consider any comparable findings.

Physical abuse was defined as being pushed, grabbed, slapped, or hit with a weapon.

Verbal abuse was defined as chronic verbal aggression, repeated insults, being sworn at, and threats at least 10 times in the preceding year.

Neglect constituted deprivation of some assistance that the elderly person needed for some important activities of daily living such as getting meals and drinks, washing and going to the toilet.

Twenty-three carers (45%) admitted to some form of abuse: 14 (27%) admitted to one type, seven (14%) to two types and two (3%) to all three types of abuse. Homer's conclusion questions the stereotyped picture of the typically abused as a frail white-haired woman over 75 years of age being abused by a well-meaning daughter driven to breakdown by stress. Different types of abuse seem to arise for different reasons. The characteristics of the abuser in physical abuse situations seemed more important than those of the abused, with alcohol consumption being greater in abusive carers. Verbal abuse seemed to have been a long-standing problem before disability. The important considerations made by Homer include:

- It is difficult to correlate abuse with physical signs (bruising).
- Social isolation and lack of services did not appear to be a risk factor.
- There is no correlation between abuse and dementia or mental impairment.
- The presence or absence of disruptive behaviours seems a potential risk factor.
- Past abusive relationships may be a risk factor.

The findings from Homer's research are most important because this is the first British study that considers causation. There is an urgency to replicate the research with a random stratified sample in order to compare the risk factors in Britain with the risk factors found by Pillemer [25].

In May 1991 the Department of Health commissioned a report on the current state of knowledge on elder abuse and neglect from the Age Concern Institute of Gerontology [26]. This report supplies an up-to-date picture of developments so far in Britain, with an analysis of American and Canadian research. McCreadie's conclusion suggests that there is a noticeable absence of British research, definitions remain unresolved, and we do not have a prevalence figure in Britain.

In order to consider the developments in the elder abuse/neglect debate thus far in Britain it is useful to use Blumer's model of social problem construction [27]. This model can be used to compare and contrast the developments in Britain against the developments in America. Blumer claims that social problems pass through five stages shown in Table 1.2.

Table 1.2 Blumer's model of social problem construction

Emergence
Legitimation
Mobilization of action
Formulation of an official plan
Implementation of the plan

The American context

Emergence

The emergence of the problem evolved through the research findings in 1979 [9–11].

Legitimation

This was agreed after the United States House Select Committee on Aging published the report, *Elder Abuse: The Hidden Problem* [12]. This legitimation was reinforced by the media, with a Harris poll of November 1981 finding 79% of the public believing elder abuse and neglect to be a serious problem, and 72% who believed it to be a major responsibility assumed by government [28].

Mobilization of action

This emerged with continued research into elder abuse and neglect, considering both the quantitative dimensions (how big is the problem) and the qualitative dimensions (what causes elder abuse and neglect and how do service practitioners intervene). The Adult Protective Services and Aging Agencies also began to involve themselves in the debate.

Formulation of an official plan

This arrived with changes in the law and continued research into the social problem of elder abuse and neglect [29].

Implementation of the plan

As of 1988 all fifty states have legislation addressing elder abuse and neglect. Forty-three states were operating mandatory statewide reporting systems, while the remaining states administer reporting systems which are not mandatory or statewide in scope [30].

The British context

Emergence

Although the first reports came from Britain research evidence is sparse; as of 1992 only Homer and Gilleard's [18] research and the prevalence study of Ogg and Bennett [17] exist. All the other work is of an anecdotal nature, clearly important, but difficult to use to legitimate the problem.

Legitimation

Numerous attempts have been made to legitimate the phenomenon, including the British Geriatrics Society Conference [22] and limited media coverage.

Mobilization of action

Action on a macro scale, including interventions of a political and policy nature, remain elusive. However, the Department of Health did commission the 1991 exploratory study, but no policy changes have occurred since its publication. At a micro level many agencies have published guidelines for practitioners to follow but central co-ordination is absent [21]. In early 1991 a group of interested practitioners began to meet informally to frame a response to elder abuse and neglect. This organization is called 'Action on Elder Abuse' and is supported by Age Concern England.

Formulation of an official plan

No official plan exists; health and social service officials continue to develop policies on an *ad hoc* basis. At this point in time there is no evaluation of the efficacy of the policies in existence.

Implementation of the plan

Outcome is awaited on this.

This state of affairs is summed up by Blumer:

Social problems are not the result of an intrinsic malfunctioning of a society but are the result of a process of definition in which a given condition is picked out and defined as a social problem. A social problem does not exist for a society unless it is recognized by that society to exist. [27]

The task of this and subsequent texts is to legitimate the social problem of elder abuse and neglect.

DEFINITIONS OF ELDER ABUSE AND NEGLECT

The main controversy which has caused research and conceptual difficulties remains the definition of elder abuse and neglect. The definition of elder abuse and neglect has probably caused more contention than any other area of concern, and the debate continues. Terminology remains in a state of flux with the latest contribution by Fulmer and O'Malley [31] arguing that 'Inadequate Care' is the term that encompasses the problem in a holistic manner. This latest contribution has developed from numerous previous definitions starting in 1979 [9–11]:

Abuse: the wilful infliction of physical pain, injury or debilitating mental anguish; unreasonable confinement; or deprivation by a caretaker of services which are necessary to maintain mental and physical health.

This definition, as with nearly all the definitions, is flawed with inconsistencies. What of the carer who inflicts pain, but not with any wilful intention (perhaps because of a lack of caring skills)? What behaviours constitute debilitating mental anguish, and more to the point from whose viewpoint, that of the abused, abuser, or service practitioner? Does unreasonable confinement suggest there is such a thing as reasonable confinement? Finally, who decides what services are necessary to maintain mental and physical health? This type of criticism, although used constructively, can be used to dismantle most definitions to date.

Table 1.3 lists some early definitions.

This lack of definitional uniformity has meant that researchers have been unable to compare and contrast results. Practitioners are also unsure how to intervene and what therapeutic

Table 1.3 Early definitions of elder abuse and neglect

Block and Sinnott [11]
Physical abuse: malnutrition, injuries, e.g. bruises, sprains,
    dislocations, abrasions or lacerations.
Psychological abuse: verbal assault, threat fear, isolation.
Material abuse: theft, misuse of money or property.
Medical abuse: withholding medication or aids required.

Lau and Kosberg [10]
Physical abuse: direct beatings, withholding personal care, food,
    medical care, lack of supervision.
Psychological abuse: verbal assaults, threats, provoking fear, isolation.
Material abuse: monetary or material theft or misuse.
Violation of rights: being forced out of one's own dwelling or forced
    into another setting.

Eastman [32]
The abuse either physical, emotional, or psychological of the elderly
by a caregiving relative on whom that elderly person is dependent.

outcomes are required and necessary. Finally, any changes
in the law that may be required are not possible because of
the lack of consistent data. The development of more precise
definitions would be a major step forward in the debate in
order to produce a solid analytical knowledge base. However,
it will serve no useful purpose to become entangled in the
difficulties that have plagued the American experience. Definitions are clearly necessary and it may be that some useful
mileage can be gained from the work of Aber and Zigler [33] in
the child abuse arena. Aber and Zigler suggest that at least
three differing sets if definitions are necessary to pursue three
differing aims. These are set out in Table 1.4.

Case-management definitions are considered within this
chapter (see Chapter 5 for legal definitions, Chapter 9 for research definitions).

The major criticism of the early definitions relates to their
specific design for research and legal purposes; Valentine and
Cash [34] make the point when they suggest:

By recognizing the necessity of different sets of definitions to
pursue different goals, the debate between the legal and
social work orientations begins to be resolved. . . . legal definitions are essential for the protection of the individual . . .

Table 1.4 Legal, case management, and research definitions (Aber and Zigler [33])

Legal definitions: to guide decision making that would specify what acts or conditions justify initial state intervention into private family life.

Case-management definitions: to guide clinical decision making that would specify eligibility for services and establish a baseline against which services are evaluated and clinical decisions about families are made.

Research definitions: to guide scientific research that would provide the basis for studying lawful causal relationships.

---

social work definitions ... for the identification and intervention ... by service practitioners.

The latest definitions considered useful in order to frame the identification and intervention for practitioners are: the concept of elder mistreatment, Johnson [35] and the concept of inadequate care, Fulmer and O'Malley [31].

Elder mistreatment

Johnson's definition of elder mistreatment falls into four sequential stages.

Stage 1: Intrinsic definition

A state of self- or other-inflicted suffering unnecessary to the maintenance of the quality of life of the older person.

Johnson argues that at this level the definition needs to be rather abstract and there are distinct advantages in using such a wide overall intrinsic definition. It is so wide that any form or degree of mistreatment may fall within the parameters. Other advantages are the ability to differentiate mistreatment from behaviours that 'may' be considered culturally acceptable. This is clearly important and research may find that different cultures may wish to have different views on what is or is not considered mistreatment. Any form of abuse may fall within this wide definition including neglect, self neglect and institutional abuse. If definitions are too restrictive then certain forms of abuse may be excluded as not falling within the parameters of the definition. This is an important point to consider in the formative stage of the development of elder abuse both as a concept and social problem.

Stage 2: Extrinsic definition

Identified as one or more behavioural manifestations, categorized as physical, psychological, sociological or legal circumstances.

This extrinsic definition names the categories of abuse; this helps to identify the behavioural manifestations which may be under scrutiny. This is clearly important from the case manager's perspective because it may suggest which service professional is best suited as primary interventionist, for example, medical, psychiatric, legal, social or other.

Stage 3: Extrinsic definition

Measured by determining the intensity and density of the behaviourial manifestations.

This definition has a potential to consider the mistreatment from the perspective of the abused person as well as the interventionist. If this is the case behaviours may be evaluated by

Table 1.5 Four domains of increasing potential danger

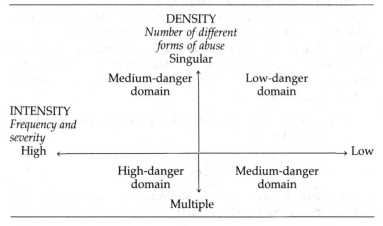

degree. For example the mistreatment may be low density (only one form of abuse) but of a high intensity (frequently happens and is severe in form). One can imagine a schema of mistreatment intensity/density. This type of schema suggests four domains of increasing potential danger (Table 1.5). This type of schema has the capacity to predict the potential degree of danger that an individual may be facing. Practitioners may then be in a position to decide the urgency or otherwise of intervention strategies.

Stage 4: Causal definition

The causal definition considers whether the abuse/neglect is active or passive. There are four domains:

Active abuse
Active neglect
Passive abuse
Passive neglect.

The causality will strongly influence the therapeutic intervention and interfaces with the continuum from:

Aggressive   ←————————————→   Passive
interventions   interventions

This model shadows the competing philosophies model [36] examined in Chapter 4. This model also considers the degree of danger the elderly find themselves facing and the speed at which the interventionist wishes to act.

The rationale put forward by Johnson for this particular approach is to move away form the 'tautological trap of using the word abuse to define abuse'. Johnson further claims that suffering is a matter of 'degree' rather than 'kind' and that in order to move forward in any attempt to reach definitional 'common ground' we must:

> . . . look at degree rather than kind and the problem rather than the parties. [35]

Inadequate care

Fulmer and O'Malley's [31] definition of inadequate care derives from their argument that:

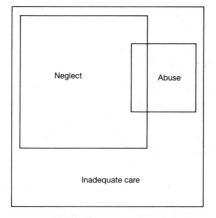

Figure 1.1 Inadequate care (Fulmer and O'Malley [31]).
Used by kind permission of Fulmer, T.T. and O'Malley, T.A. *Inadequate Care of the Elderly: A Health Care Perspective on Abuse and Neglect.* Springer Publishing Company Inc., New York 10012 (1987) [31].

it is easier to reach a consensus on what constitutes adequate and inadequate care than it is to agree upon what is acceptable and unacceptable behaviour within families or among professionals (see Figure 1.1).

The other dimension relates to the labelling of abuse; it is easier to define a case as inadequate than to label a case as elder abuse/neglect. Fulmer and O'Malley also claim that most definitions are too restrictive (as did Johnson previously) and have evolved from a research perspective rather than a patient care perspective. By opening out the definition, all cases of abuse and neglect can be considered to fall under the global definition of inadequate care with abuse being sub-defined as:

. . . actions of a caretaker that create unmet needs for the elderly person.

and neglect being defined as:

. . . the failure of an individual responsible for care-taking to respond adequately to established needs for care.

Within both definitions 'needs' may consist of food, shelter, clothing, supportive relationships, freedom from harassment or threats of violence and the requirements of activities of daily living. As with Johnson's [35] definition, the qualitative dimension of unmet need can be considered alongside the quantity of need. Both Johnson's and Fulmer and O'Malley's definitions see the perception of the abused person as crucial:

> ... although society can develop general descriptions of the behaviors it considers unacceptable, only the elderly person can decide if those definitions apply in his or her individual case. In a sense the elderly person can render a definition of abuse or neglect meaningless. [31]

THEORIES OF ELDER ABUSE AND NEGLECT

The early British reports on elder abuse and neglect conceptualized the phenomenon as the result of the stressed-carer hypothesis. Carers, predominantly female, who had agreed (sometimes reluctantly) to care for an elderly person had been driven to abuse because of the continued pressure and stress of caring. This picture was reinforced by Eastman's study of social service staff attitudes to elder abuse and neglect [37]. The actual cause of abuse was considered mainly to be stress related, with 80% considering stress to be the overriding factor (Table 1.6).

The scenario of the stressed carer was difficult to dispute because research was not available to offer any other conceptual frameworks. However, it quickly became apparent that not all carers abused or neglected the elderly they cared for, although many of these carers would admit to varying degrees of stress. One survey of 3000 carers [38] found 88% of women carers said that: they suffered from stress through being a carer

Table 1.6 Causation of elder abuse/neglect. Factors in order of importance. From Eastman [37]

1. Stress
2. Psychological problems
3. Lack of community resources (Refusal to accept)
4. Alcohol problems
5. Lack of community resource (Inadequate resource)
6. Revenge

Table 1.7 Risk factors for elder abuse/neglect

Intraindividual dynamic (Psychopathology of the abuser).
Intergenerational transmission of violence (Cycle of violence theory).
Dependency and exchange relationships between abuser and abused.
External stress.
Social isolation.

as well as working, while 44% of men said that they suffered stress for the same reason.

When Pillemer and Finkelhor's prevalence figure suggested that 3.2 cases in 100 suffered abuse [24] the pertinent question to ask was:

What is unique about this particular 3.2% both from the perspective of abused and abuser?

The answer came from American research, albeit substantiated in the work of Homer [18] in Britain. A theoretical review of the literature on elder abuse and neglect suggests five areas that consistently emerge as risk factors (Table 1.7).

In order to test whether these hypothetical risk factors hold true a study of physically abused elders was conducted as part of the Three-Models Project [25]. The research compared 42 abused elders with a matched non-abused group of 42 elders.

Intraindividual dynamics

The first risk factor tested was the hypothesis that abusive behaviour is linked to some form of pathology on the part of the abuser. Two questions were asked relating to mental or emotional problems on the part of their carer. The abused elderly reported substantial higher levels of pathology on the part of the carer: 79% compared with only 24% in the non-abused group.

Questions about psychiatric hospitalization were also asked; again the relatives of the abused elderly had reported levels of 35.7% compared to 7.1% in the non-abused group. Alcohol abuse was also considered, with the caseworkers of both the abused and non-abused being asked:

To the best of your knowledge is (relative) an alcoholic?

The abusers were again substantially more likely to be alcohol dependent (45.2% compared to 7.1%). These findings clearly suggest that mental status (illness past or present) and alcohol abuse need to be considered as high-risk factors for elder abuse and neglect. Similar findings by Homer and Gilleard [18] would substantiate these findings.

Intergenerational transmission of violence

The concept of intergenerational transmission of violence was considered by asking the respondents:

> How did you usually tend to punish (child) when he or she was a child/teenager?

Two codes were used for replies, either:

- physical punishment mentioned, or
- physical punishment not mentioned.

Only one respondent mentioned using physical punishment. This question was followed by:

> How frequently have you used physical punishment in the year you used it most, ranging from never to 20 times?

No significant differences were found in this variable between the abused and non-abused groups. Pillemer suggests that this data is limited and does not support the hypothesis that abusers were victims of abuse by their parents. Pillemer further suggests that methodologically the survey format may not be the ideal way to gain information on punishment and abuse of children. The traditional rhyme, although anonymous, in the introduction of Schlesinger and Schlesinger's text clearly needs more research to justify its inclusion in many elder abuse texts:

> When I was a laddy, I lived with my granny, and many a hiding me granny gied me.
> Now I am a man, and I live with my granny, and I do to my granny what she did to me. [39]

Dependency

Dependency has traditionally been seen as a potentate of stress, with the view that:

Increased dependency = Stress = Abuse/neglect

However, the alternative hypothesis suggesting that abuse and neglect may be caused by an imbalance in the power relationship with the abuser dependent on the abused is gaining ground [40]. Elders that were abused were not considered more functionally disabled and ill than the control group, and surprisingly in certain areas were less impaired. The abused group were not more dependent on their carer than the non-abused group in activities of daily living (ADL). In support of the imbalance of power relationship theory, the abusers were more likely to be dependent on their victims than the non-abused.

Stress

External stress did not seem to be a significant risk factor, other than to say that three particular stressors emerged in the abused group:

someone moving in with the abuser
someone leaving the household
someone getting arrested.

However, the abuser was responsible for the event because the shared living became unbearable. Therefore if these three questions are not considered, stress items between groups would not differ.

Social isolation

With the final risk factor of social isolation the abused group scored fewer contacts (family members and friends) than the non-abused group (36% and 17% respectively). The abused group considered their relationships to be less satisfactory (39% and 20% respectively). These results do not suggest that isolation causes elder abuse and neglect and Pillemer claims that abusers may break down social support structures because of their behaviour towards visitors.

In essence this particular piece of research suggests that the concept of elder abuse as 'Caregiver Abuse' may need to be substituted for the concept of elder abuse and neglect as another facet of 'Domestic Abuse'. A move away from the characteristics of the abused towards the characteristics of the abuser may also be necessary in order to begin to conceptualize the nature of elder abuse as a social problem.

REFERENCES

1. Department of Health (1989) *Caring for People: Community Care in the Next Decade and Beyond.* Cm 849. HMSO.
2. *Social Trends 21* (1991) Central Statistical Office. HMSO.
3. Kosberg, J. (1988) Preventing elder abuse: identification of high risk factors prior to placement decisions. *The Gerontologist,* 28 (1), 43–50.
4. Leroux, T.G. and Petrunik M. (1990) The construction of elder abuse as a social problem: A Canadian perspective. *International Journal of Health Services,* 20 (4), 651–63.
5. Sumner, W.G. (1960) *Folkways: A Study of the Sociological Importance of Usage, Manners, Customs, Mores and Morals.* The New American Library, New York.
6. Baker, A.A. (1975) Granny battering. *Modern Geriatrics.* August 5, (8), 20–4.
7. The Concise Oxford Dictionary (1991) Oxford University Press, Oxford.
8. Burston, G. (1977) Do your elderly patients live in fear of being battered. *Modern Geriatrics,* 7 (5), 54–5.
9. O'Malley, H. *et al.* (1979) *Elder Abuse in Massachusetts: A Survey of Professionals and Paraprofessionals.* Legal Research and Services for the Elderly, Boston.
10. Lau, E. and Kosberg, J. (1979) Abuse of the elderly by informal caregivers. *Aging,* 229, 10–15.
11. Block, M. and Sinnott, J. (1979) *The Battered Elder Syndrome: An Exploratory Study.* University of Maryland, Center on Aging, College Park.
12. United States Congress House Select Committee on Aging (1980) *Elder Abuse: The Hidden Problem.* Government Printing Office, Washington DC.
13. Edwards, S. (1982) Granny battering: a problem that doctors are failing to detect? *Medical News,* 14, 16–18.
14. Traynor, J. and Hasnip, L. (1984) Sometimes she makes me want to hit her. *Community Care.* August 2nd, 20–1.
15. Eastman, M. (1984) Honour thy father and thy mother. *Community Care.* January 26th, 17–20.
16. *Hansard* (1982) Written answer, 26th November.
17. Ogg, J. and Bennett, G. (1992) Elderly abuse in Britain. *British Medical Journal,* 305, 998–9.
18. Homer, A. and Gilleard, C. (1990) Abuse of elderly people by their carers. *British Medical Journal,* 301, 1359–62.
19. Eastman, M. (1984) *Old Age Abuse.* Age Concern England.

20. Department of Health and Social Security (1985) *Performance Indicator Packages*. HMSO, London.
21. Kingston, P. (1991) Elder abuse. In *Elder Abuse. An Exploratory Study* (ed. McCreadie, C.). Age Concern Institute of Gerontology, King's College London.
22. Tomlin, S. (1989) *Abuse of elderly people: an unnecessary and preventable problem*. British Geriatrics Society.
23. British Geriatrics Society (1990) *Scream but don't Abuse*.
24. Pillemer, K. and Finkelhor, D. (1988) The prevalence of elder abuse: a random survey sample. *The Gerontologist*, 28 (1), 51–7.
25. Pillemer, K. (1986) Risk factors in elder abuse: results from a case-control study. In *Elder Abuse: Conflict in the Family* (ed. Pillemer, K. and Wolf, R.), Auburn House, Dover, MA.
26. McCreadie, C. (ed.) (1991) *Elder Abuse: An Exploratory Study*. Age Concern Institute of Gerontology, King's College London.
27. Blumer, H. (1971) Social problems as collective behaviour. *Social Problems*, 18 (3), 298–306.
28. Harris, L. (1981) Americans believe Government should take major responsibility in coping with the abuse problem. News Release. *The Harris Survey*.
29. Cabness, J. (1989) The emergency shelter: a model for building the self-esteem of abused elders. *Journal of Elder Abuse and Neglect*, 1 (2), 71–82.
30. American Public Welfare Association/NASUA (1986) *A comprehensive analysis of state policy and practice related to elder abuse: A focus on role activities of state level agencies, interagency co-ordination efforts, public education/information campaigns*. Washington DC.
31. Fulmer, T. and O'Malley, T.A. (1987) *Inadequate Care of the Elderly: A Health Care Perspective on Abuse and Neglect*. Springer, New York.
32. Eastman, M. (1982) Granny battering: a hidden problem. *Community Care*. May 27th.
33. Aber, J.L. and Zigler, E. (1981) Developmental considerations in the definition of child maltreatment. *New Directions for Child Development*, 11, 1–29.
34. Valentine, D. and Cash, T. (1986) A definitional discussion of elder mistreatment. *Journal of Gerontological Social Work*, 9 (3), 17–28.
35. Johnson, T.F. (1986) Critical issues in the definition of elder mistreatment. In *Elder Abuse: Conflict in the Family* (ed. Pillemer, K. and Wolf, R.), Auburn House, Dover, MA.
36. Rosenfield, A. and Newberger, E.H. (1977) Compassion vs. control: conceptual and practical pitfalls in the broadened definition of child abuse. *Journal of the American Medical Association*, 237, 2086–8.
37. Eastman, M. (1984) At worst just picking up the pieces. *Community Care*, February 2nd.
38. Opportunities for women (1990) *Carers at Work*. Opportunities for Women, London.

39. Schlesinger, B. and Schlesinger, R. (1988) *Abuse of the Elderly: Issues and Annotated Bibliography*. University of Toronto Press.
40. Wolf, R.S., Strugnell, C. and Godkin, M. (1982) *Preliminary Findings from the Three-Models Project on Elderly Abuse*. University of Massachusetts, University Center on Aging, Worcester, MA.

2

The abused and the abuser

FOCUS ON THE ABUSER

The focus of attention in the abuse situation has until recently been dominated by the characteristics of the potentially abused person. This spotlighting of the abused is about to alter, however, shifting more to the abuser. This change in emphasis is due to the extensive research work that has been carried out in the United States and reports beginning to appear in the UK medical and social literature.

'CLASSIC' VICTIM

In 1988 the British Geriatrics Society held the first national conference on the topic of elder abuse. Over 400 delegates (including doctors involved in health care of the elderly, psychiatrists, GPs, social workers and nurses) heard the early tentative comments from professionals interested in the field. The report following the conference outlined the characteristics of the classic victim [1]. These are listed in Table 2.1.

A picture is painted of a physically frail old woman, dependent on help for many of the activities of daily living. A typical illness process producing such a situation would be Parkinson's disease. As the disease progresses the lifeline of communication may be lost, with incessant drooling, difficulty speaking, and the onset of dementia. Finally continence is lost (either involuntarily due to brain damage or voluntarily due to the inability to get to the toilet fast enough). The mind's eye image of total and utter dependency is complete – the so-called archetypal victim.

Key issues appear to be advanced old age, being female, living at home with adult carers, being physically and mentally impaired, being overweight (i.e. hard to lift), immobile and

Table 2.1 'Classic' elderly abuse victim

Elderly (over the age of 75)
Female
Roleless
Functionally impaired
Lonely and fearful
Living at home with an adult offspring

incontinent, with negative personality traits (biting, hitting out, spitting, smearing faeces, masturbating, etc.). This process of trying to define the classic victim's characteristics is useful if research confirms that these characteristics are indeed accurate.

We tend to think that they must be true because we can all identify with and empathize with this caring situation and the enormous strain that must result (in part legitimating but not condoning any subsequent abusive episodes) – the victim-blaming concept [2]. Problems arise, however, when research findings muddy rather than clear the picture. Pillemer and Wolf are two highly respected researchers in this topic in the US. In their book *Elder Abuse: Conflict in the Family* [3] 42 physically abused elderly people were compared with a non-abused control group. Their findings are summarized in the key sentence: '. . . the notion that physical elder abuse results from the strain of caring for a dependent old person found little support' (p. 261). In this study the victims did not suffer from more illness or disability and were not more dependent in terms of their need for help in the activities of daily living. These findings appear to be substantiated by the work of Homer and Gilleard in the UK [4] where '. . . the lack of as-sociation between abuse and the diagnosis of dementia or degree of mental impairment of the patient is noteworthy.'

The situation is thus far more complex than was originally presumed. It appears therefore that there may not be a con-venient 'victim' classification process. Certainly the physically and mentally frail old person still predominates in the published literature. However, that image is being replaced with the view that any elderly person may be at risk because it is not so much victim characteristics that are important as those of the carer.

This can be conceptually difficult for as soon as the word 'carer' is used we introduce the notion of dependency on the part of the victim, and therefore dependency must be part of the dynamics in abuse. If an elderly person who is not dependent is abused (because of the characteristics of the abuser) then many people see this in terms of domestic/family violence.

The Carers National Association describes carers as 'those whose lives are restricted by the need to take responsibility for the care of someone who is mentally ill, mentally handicapped, physically disabled or whose health is impaired by sickness or old age.' The report on the British Geriatrics Society conference describes carers thus:

> They are people like you or me, with no specific training in caring or nursing, yet they have to perform the duties of a nurse 24 hours a day, week in, week out, often single handed. Most carers are naturally compassionate people; it is the constant pressure on them that may make frustration and anger overspill into violence. [1]

The Government have also come up with a definition which is typically neutral. A carer is:

> a person who is not employed to provide the care in question by any body in the exercise of its function under any enactment. . . . the dependency relationship exceeds that implicit in normally dependent relationships between family members. [5]

Table 2.2 Factors predisposing to abuse by carers

1. Physical and mental dependence on a key member of the family
2. Poor communication or a breakdown in communication
3. Considerable change in a carer's lifestyle
4. Perception of carer towards dependence of older person
5. Frequent visits to general practitioners by the informal carers to talk about their problems
6. Role reversal
7. History of falls and minor injuries
8. Triggering behaviour – incident that acts as a catalyst, inducing loss of control
9. Carer and dependants' apathy
10. Cramped or substandard living conditions
11. Isolation of the household

Table 2.3 Risk factors for inadequate care

1. Those with chronic progressive disabling illnesses that impair function and create care needs that exceed or will exceed their caretaker's ability to meet them, such as:
   - Dementia (Alzheimer's disease, multi-infarct dementia, etc.)
   - Parkinson's disease
   - Severe arthritis (osteo and rheumatoid)
   - Severe cardiac disease
   - Severe chronic obstructive pulmonary disease (COPD), e.g. chronic bronchitis or emphysema)
   - Adult-onset diabetes mellitus (AODM)
   - Recurrent strokes.
2. Those with progressive impairments who are without informal support from family or neighbours, or whose caretakers manifest signs of 'burn-out'.
3. Those with a personal history of substance abuse or violent behaviour, or a family member with the same.
4. Those who live with a family in which there is a history of child or spouse abuse.
5. Those with family members who are financially dependent on them.
6. Those residing in institutions that have a history of providing substandard care.
7. Those whose caretakers are under sudden increased stress due for example to loss of a job, health or spouse.

PREDISPOSING FACTORS

In the same vein some attempt has been made to identify the main predisposing factors leading to carers abusing [6]. Table 2.2 lists these.

The main thrust not only emphasizes the dependence of the elderly person but also the needs of the carers and their actions (such as the 'cry for help' visits to the general practitioner). The US literature has begun to open out this intensely focused scenario. Fulmer and O'Malley (who use the term 'inadequate care' to describe possible abuse) have devised a list of risk factors associated with inadequate care [7]; see Table 2.3.

'INADEQUATE CARE' RISK FACTORS

Fulmer and O'Malley obviously still stress the issues of dependency inherent in the literature but begin a shift of attention away from the elderly subject and subtly towards the carers. They list 'burn-out' as a risk factor. This American term is gaining increased usage in the UK. In this context it implies a loss of the normal social inhibiting mechanisms that help mould one's behaviour. A couple may want to argue whilst out with friends but in front of others the most that usually happens is a 'wait until we get home' through clenched teeth and a rather 'frosty' atmosphere! The same couple towards the end of a deteriorating exhausting relationship exhibit 'burn-out' by hurling insults and unkind remarks at each other regardless of who else is present. A similar picture is seen in abuse. As the relationship deteriorates, previously hidden actions or words (the painful tugging up from a chair, a hard push in the back to hurry someone along, or a tactless insensitive remark) occur in the presence of others, often visiting health-care workers.

Fulmer and O'Malley also introduce the concept of violence into the domestic setting and the key aspect of the role of drugs and alcohol (client or carer) as important agents. Family violence has spawned many books in its own right. The debate continues as to the appropriateness of calling a situation 'spouse abuse' one day and 'elder abuse' the day after a 60th birthday. Certainly violence as a sociological phenomenon gets it featured as one of the aetiological theories (Chapter 1). There is a possibility that transgenerational violence occurs and that there are situations where children are abused who then go on to indulge in spouse abuse and abuse their own children and later become the recipients of abuse themselves as elderly people. At this point in time our survey tools are too crude and are probably not sensitive enough to pick up this problem. When found, the violence appears to be endemic in these families and acts almost as an unusual form of communication. The violence is habitual and exacerbated by the use of drugs, especially alcohol.

One can, however, distinguish between those groups where violence is almost a way of life and where the abuse of a wife has imperceptibly become abuse of an older person, from those situations where a carer with violent tendencies, psychopathic behaviour or substance abuse newly finds him or herself in a caring role – indeed forced into a role with care tasks totally beyond their ability. Sociopathic and psychopathic behaviour and addictions to alcohol and drugs are no respecters of class or race; indeed,

> . . . research to date has found cases of abuse and neglect in all social and economic strata, in rural and urban settings, in all religious groups, and in all races. [7]

THE THREE-MODEL PROJECT

The term 'non-normal caregiver' was used by Pillemer and Wolf to highlight this focusing of attention on the carer and its possible importance as an aetiological factor in cases of abuse [3]. Further information was provided by one of the most important research projects carried out in this field. The Three-Model Project supported by the US National Institute on Aging involved three separate research projects: a random sample prevalence survey to determine the extent of elderly abuse in a given geographical area, improving mechanisms for reporting cases and investigating treatment and prevention programmes, and the design of social and legal remedies to restore the rights and wellbeing of the abused elderly. The three sites selected were Boston, Massachusetts; Syracuse, New York; and Rhode Island.

The Boston arm of the study provided the first large-scale random survey of elder abuse and neglect [8]. The data is of great relevance to the abused/abuser question as a non-abused control group was used to test (as Pillemer puts it):

> the wide accepted proposition that such abuse results from the burden and stress placed on those caring for infirm and dependent elderly people. [8]

Over 2000 elderly people were surveyed in a two-stage interview process. Three major areas of interest were identified: physical abuse, psychological abuse and neglect. These categories were then given a working research 'definition'. The survey revealed a rate of 32 maltreated elderly per 1000 (a prevalence rate of 3.2%). Physical violence was the most common form of abuse, followed by psychological abuse and neglect. The data on the victims showed that rates of abuse were similar for the 'young' old (under 75) as for the 'old' old and that there were no differences in religious, economic or educational background. Those living with a spouse and one other carer were especially vulnerable, as too were those in poor health. Roughly equal numbers of abused men and women were found, but the women were more seriously abused.

A further study involving a non-abused control group analysed the characteristics of the abusers [9]. In this study more women than men were abused and the majority were over 75. Psychological abuse predominated and poor health was not a significant risk factor. However, a significantly higher percentage of the caregivers in abusive situations were men (71%), over half the abusers being husbands or sons. The data on the psychological status of the abuser revealed that 41% of caregivers had a history of mental or emotional illness (compared to 5% for controls) and that alcohol abuse occurred in one-third of the cases, but not at all in the comparison group.

CONCLUSIONS

What do these various studies tell us? They indicate that the early investigators used small unrepresentative samples, omitted control groups, and relied on loose definitions. The initial stereotyped plot with the victim depicted as female and 'old' old with physical and mental disabilities being abused by a caring but overburdened daughter has had to undergo rewriting. As Wolf puts it, 'the concept [has] evolved into a much more varied set of characters and relationships' [9]. The Boston survey indicates that a large proportion of elder abuse is spouse abuse. Pillemer interprets this as due to the fact that spouses are more likely to be present in elderly households, hence the opportunities for abusive behaviour are greater. It also indicated that men can be subjected to abuse.

As the star emphasizing caregiver stress as the main risk factor for abuse wanes, so the one highlighting the role of psychological illness and alcohol abuse in abusive carers is in the ascendant. Wolf [10] takes the analysis of all the research work even further. She believes that at least three different profiles emerge:

1. Victims of physical and psychological abuse tend to be physically well (reasonable activities of daily living scores) but have emotional problems. The abusers have a history of

alcoholism and/or mental illness, live with the victim, and are dependent upon them financially.
2. Victims of neglect are usually very old, and mentally and physically impaired with little social support. The carer finds the victim a great source of stress.
3. Victims of financial (material) abuse tend to be unmarried with limited social contacts/networks. The abusers have financial problems sometimes traceable to a history of drug or alcohol abuse.

Above is a distillation of over 10 years of work in the US. One cannot do the same for the UK work – there is so little of it. Research is obviously needed in the UK to see if the results are similar. Many researchers feel that the caregiver stress hypothesis will find little empirical confirmation in the UK as well. Indeed some find its persistence as a theory remarkable, a sort of victim-blaming mentality [2]. This issue has parallels with domestic violence where feminists demonstrated that the phenomenon was labelled 'battered wives' and not 'violent husbands' [11].

If UK research does confirm the US findings the implications would be profound. A simple correlation with US prevalence rates would result in a figure of approximately 280 000 elderly UK people at risk. No one would surely deny the continued need to try to relieve some of the burden of caring. This help must be in as many and as diverse forms as possible (practical, financial and legal) and must expand from its current miserly base. New programmes of specific help will be needed, however, to tackle the issue effectively. The roles of psychological counselling, victim and carer support groups, victim advocacy schemes, greater police involvement, and legal assistance and legislation have yet to be debated.

REFERENCES

1. Tomlinson, S. (1988) *Abuse of elderly people: an unnecessary and preventable problem.* Public Information Report. British Geriatrics Society. September.
2. Traynor, J. and Hasnip, L. (1984) Sometimes she makes me want to hit her. *Community Care,* August 2nd, 20–1.
3. Pillemer, K.A. and Wolf, R.S. (ed.) (1986) *Elder Abuse: Conflict in the Family.* Auburn House, Dover, MA.

4. Homer, A. and Gilleard, C. (1990) Abuse of elderly people by their carers. *British Medical Journal*, 301, 1359–62.
5. *Community Care in the Next Decade and Beyond*. (1990) Appendix B/1 HMSO.
6. Eastman, M. (1984) *Old Age Abuse*. Age Concern. June.
7. Fulmer, T.T. and O'Malley, T.A. (1987) *Inadequate Care of the Elderly*. Springer Publishing Co., New York.
8. Pillemer, K.A. and Finklehor, D. (1988) The prevalence of elder abuse. *The Gerontologist*, 28, 51–7.
9. Godkin, M.A., Wolf, R.S. and Pillemer, K.A. (1989) A case comparison analysis of elder abuse and neglect. *International Journal of Aging and Human Development*, 28 (3), 207–25.
10. Wolf, R.S. (1989) *Testimony before the Subcommittee of Human Services. Select Committee on Aging. US House of Representatives. Hearings on Elder Abuse*. National Committee for the Prevention of Elder Abuse. University of Massachusetts Medical Center, Worcester, MA.
11. *Domestic Violence*. (1989) HMSO.

3

Recognition and assessment of abuse

The recognition of elder abuse (inadequate care) is for the most part still at a very basic level. In cases of physical abuse fairly gross changes need to be present (Figure 3.1) before any degree of certainty is reached, although more subtle features such as finger marks due to harsh gripping are now being recognized (Figure 3.2). The symptoms and signs associated with psychological abuse and sexual abuse are still much less well authenticated than similar situations concerning children. There are two major reasons behind this anomalous situation.

Only a few decades ago any form of child abuse was considered rare. Case reports began appearing in the medical press of a few children with two or more fractures of different ages and indeed bruises at different stages of healing (as indicated by colour) possibly caused by parental/carer violence. Sexual abuse was practically unheard of and not given conscious thought by most clinicians. Gradually Accident and Emergency units around the country started 'seeing' the condition, and social workers and paediatricians began the long hard learning curve that has resulted in our current knowledge base. How simple, naive and inaccurate those initial assessment procedures now seem with the benefit of hindsight and the extensive research and indeed frequent scandals that have occurred. The information we have now on child abuse has been obtained after years of professional–client interaction and multifaceted research initiatives, both sometimes painful but necessary processes. A problem was recognized and solutions sought. This process has barely started with elder abuse.

The second reason behind the anomaly in the different knowledge bases between child and elder abuse is more

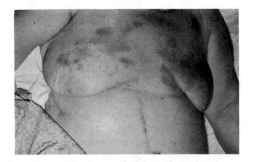

Figure 3.1 Gross changes revealing elder abuse/inadequate care.

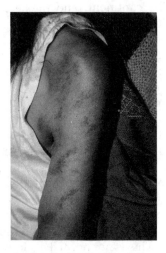

Figure 3.2 Finger marks due to harsh gripping.

complex. Children have very well-defined and clear developmental stages. Professionals dealing with normal healthy children have their own experience and numerous charts and guidelines to indicate fairly accurately what children should be achieving, growth norms, etc. Children also get seen frequently by all sorts of people, health visitors, district nurses, GP, teacher, etc. who all have the opportunity to spot abnormal symptoms and signs. These range from physical pointers (failure to thrive, unexplainable skin marks, etc.) to abnormal behaviour (sudden-onset bedwetting, undue fearfulness or precocious sexual behaviour). A vast library of information is now available to help professionals decide what is normal and what is abnormal in a child's developmental progress.

The same is not the case for the elderly and indeed will prove much more difficult to establish. The physiological changes that occur with ageing are not well known even by most health care professionals dealing with the elderly. Gerontology, the study of ageing, is still a very new science. Normal ageing appears to be a much more gradual and benign process than was originally thought. It involves slow and almost imperceptible declines from maturity onwards (30–40!) in most of the body processes. Thus muscle strength and power, lung and heart function, etc., all gradually decline, but a normal fit 80-year-old is mobile, continent, and intellectually the match of anyone younger (usually because of the benefit of experience). This differs markedly from the generally held view concerning the elderly, i.e. of people entering a second childhood, intellectually frail, falling repeatedly, incontinent and immobile. This scenario occurs but it is as the result of disease, i.e. abnormal not normal ageing.

This distinction between what is normal ageing and what is disease is crucial to the laying down of a knowledge base in the field of recognition and assessment of possible cases of abuse/inadequate care. A few areas can be highlighted to show the dilemmas confronting workers in this topic.

As we age our skin undergoes subtle changes but these are in fact at a microscopic level. Most people, however, equate ageing skin changes with wrinkles, warts and 'liver spots' as seen in Figure 3.3. This is not normal ageing. These changes are

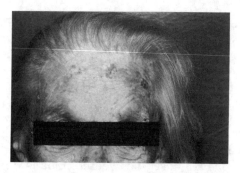

Figure 3.3 Typical skin changes caused by ultraviolet light rather than normal ageing.

due to the sun's ultraviolet light, and hence sunbathing hastens these events, causing wrinkles to occur more severely and at a much earlier age than one's 'family tree' (i.e. genetics) would have warranted. Wrinkles are only cosmetic, other skin changes have a potentially much more serious effect. In most elderly people the unavoidable exposure to the sun of the forearms (and legs in women) results in the skin becoming thinner. A substance called collagen acts as a scaffold for blood vessels just under the surface; this too is affected and supports the blood vessels less well. This means that minor trauma (a knock) can cause a blood vessel to break, resulting in a bruise. The mechanism for clearing away bruises is less effective as we age, and hence they stay around for longer periods.

The situation is made even more complex by some elderly people being more affected than others. A small group go on to develop what is known as the transparent skin syndrome. In this condition the skin becomes paper thin (caused by an excessive reaction to sunlight over the years). However, the thinning is so severe that the skin will bruise and even break on normal handling, i.e. touching and dressing. The results can look appalling and suspicious (Figure 3.4). Thus bruising in the elderly is not a straightforward issue and cannot be used as a definitive sign in elder abuse.

Falls and incontinence are two conditions that occur commonly in the very elderly. They are not part of normal ageing, but the elderly person's signalling of an underlying disease process. Investigation will hopefully result in disease processes

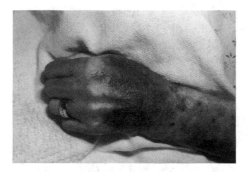

Figure 3.4 Suspicious marks caused by transparent skin syndrome rather than abuse.

being found and treated and, for the majority of people, alleviation if not cure. Falls and incontinence need to be recognized as illnesses before proper help can be obtained. In the few cases where help is not curative, everyone should be made aware of the problem and coping strategies organized. If the connection between falls, incontinence, and illness is not made the resulting injuries and bruises and the inevitable poor hygiene can easily lead to the mistaken assumption of abuse/ inadequate care (see Chapter 5).

The physiological changes that can occur in ageing and disease will thus have great bearing in the recognition and assessment procedures. Purely physical signs should be interpreted with great caution until the knowledge base has been built up as a result of experience and research. The assessment procedure for a possibly abused elderly person must be as holistic as possible. The time-honoured approach of history taking and physical examination is somewhat modified to gain even more information.

In the US the professionals working in the field are far more confident of their recognition and assessment criteria than we in the UK. Alerting features for the doctor have been outlined by Cochran and Petrose [1]. They include any discrepancy between an injury and the history, inappropriate injuries, conflicting stories, vague explanations, or denial. There may be bizarre or inappropriate explanations, or insistence from a client that an injury is severe when no injury exists (presumably as a way of getting professional help). A long delay in reporting the injury is also suspicious. A story of an elderly person being 'accident prone' should be cause for attention as should histories of previous injuries, untreated old injuries, and multiple injuries especially at various stages of healing. Repeat attendances of clients to Accident and Emergency departments from the same institution should also trigger concern.

US doctors are also alerted by injuries in areas usually covered by clothing, injuries consistent with the shape of a weapon or bruising/laceration on the lips (from forced feeding and gagging). Whiplash injuries can occur from shaking, and sexual abuse can result in laceration, bruising and bleeding of the rectum and genitalia (see Chapter 7). Fractures in the usually immobile, and alopecia (hair loss) and bleeding from hair pulling are other suspicious signs. Difficult conditions

Table 3.1 Manifestations of inadequate care

Abrasions	Dehydration
Lacerations	Malnutrition
Contusions	Inappropriate clothing
Burns	Poor hygiene
Freezing	Oversedation
Depression	Over- or undermedication
Fractures	Untreated medical problems
Sprains	Behaviour that endangers client or others
Dislocations	Failure to meet legal obligations
Decubitus sores (pressure sores)	

to establish the causation include malnutrition, dehydration, weight loss and pressure sore formation. A history of previous physical abuse of a patient and occasionally previous suicide attempts should also alert the doctor.

Fulmer and O'Malley [2] list the manifestations of inadequate care for health care professionals (Table 3.1).

There are said to be other physical indicators of abuse not shared with neglect [2] (Table 3.2).

The most common presentations of inadequate care usually involve combinations of symptoms and signs, e.g. poor nutrition, poorly controlled medical problems, frequent falls, and confusion. Thus the GP, district nurse, health visitor, and casualty officer will often be the first people to be presented with the diagnostic dilemmas. Less often legal, Social Services, or the police are the agencies first involved usually because of financial or housing problems. The presence of one or more of the list of manifestations of inadequate care obviously does not establish a diagnosis of abuse or neglect; the same findings can occur in ill frail elderly people as part of their chronic health process. In spite of this the presence of these symptoms or signs should alert the attending professionals to the possibility of inadequate care.

Occasionally elderly persons themselves report that they have been abused. This usually happens when they have formed a close enough relationship with a member of staff to divulge their worries. Two groups of staff in particular are in the position to form these close bonds – nursing and therapy.

Table 3.2 Physical indicators of abuse not shared with neglect

Unexplained bruises and welts:
    Face, lips and mouth
    Torso, back, buttocks, thighs
    In various stages of healing
    Clustered, forming regular patterns
    Reflecting shape of article used (cord, buckle)
    On several different surface areas
    Regularly appear after absence, weekend or holidays
Unexplained burns:
    Cigar, cigarette, especially on soles, palms, back or buttocks
    Immersion burns (sock-like on feet, glove-like on hands, doughnut
      shaped on buttocks or genitalia)
    Patterned like electric burner, iron, etc.
    Rope burns on arms, legs, neck or torso
Unexplained fractures:
    To skull, nose, facial structure
    In various stages of healing
    Multiple or spinal fractures
Unexplained lacerations or abrasions:
    To mouth, lips, gums or eyes
    To external genitalia
Sexual abuse:
    Difficulty in walking or sitting
    Torn, stained or bloody underclothing
    Pain or itching in the genital area
    Bruises or bleeding in external genitalia, vaginal or anal areas
    Venereal disease

The periods of time spent in close proximity, the detailed explaining of procedures, and the striving to reach rehabilitation goals means that very special relationships are formed, allowing for the discussion of otherwise unvoiced concerns. Fulmer and O'Malley then recommend that the history taking be expanded and specific questions asked. This will involve enquiring about theft or misappropriation of resources, about possible enforced social isolation or confinement. The client will need to be asked about any threats or coercion, the use of restraints or locking in a room, any actual episodes of battering, sexual abuse, threats of punishment or the withholding of food, clothing or privileges to enforce behaviour.

SOCIAL ASSESSMENT

This aspect of assessment may require many interviews over a period of time and thus the procedure can be very time consuming. One interview technique involves the 5 Ps:

Privacy (Interview the carers separately)
Pacing (Client and carers should not be rushed)
Planning (A set list of questions and procedures to be worked through)
Pitch (Voice tone and attitude to impart trust and confidence)
Punctuality (When meeting clients at home or with a pre-arranged interview in an institution)

Locally produced guidelines may help with interview techniques.

As far as possible only pertinent and appropriate information should be collected and where possible should include financial details. Quinn and Tomita [3] describe the importance of enquiring about a typical day. This naturally leads into a verbal assessment of the client's ability to perform activities of daily living. This may need to be very detailed, giving both client and carer an opportunity to describe their perceived and actual difficulties. This task may be best performed by an experienced therapist; one useful tool may be the Cost of Care Index [4]. Quinn and Tomita also describe the need to explore the client's expectations about care, getting information on recent crises in the family as well as the sensitive areas of alcohol problems, drug use/abuse, illnesses and behaviour problems within the household or family members.

The client's current mental status should always be ascertained before detailed questioning begins. This will have to be explained (see the section on the elderly mentally infirm) as mentally competent people can get irritated when having the memory assessed. Failure to assess memory can lead to great difficulties later. Where there seems to be an indication of some unusual circumstances, more in-depth questions should follow, tact and accuracy remaining paramount.

The most sensitive questioning area is that of actual abusive episodes, detailing verbal and physical incidents. Specific questions relating to the episodes may need to be asked for greater clarification. Interviewing the caregiver is another emotionally demanding situation. Different interview techniques are used by various professionals and some have developed high levels of skill (social work). Many people rely on the use of a formal protocol – an aide memoire to formalize the interview situation.

SCREENING INSTRUMENTS

Formal protocols (screening instruments) for use in suspected cases of elder abuse are being developed in the US. They can be very lengthy to complete but are thus thorough and provide detailed information on which to base reports regarding alleged abuse/inadequate care. One such instrument is the elder assessment instrument (EAI) [5]. The EAI has eight sections and is designed and arranged to elicit symptoms and signs by health care professionals, the total forming a small booklet.

Section 1 consists of demographic data (age, sex, address, next of kin). It also includes an assessment of the client's mental state.

Section 2 is concerned with a general assessment – hygiene, nutrition, skin integrity and clothing (with ranges from very good to very poor).

Section 3 involves a physical assessment of bruises, contractures, pressure sores, lacerations etc. (with ranges of definite evidence through to no evidence). Other screening instruments in this section include a human figure chart (back and front) so that accurate location of marks/bruises can be made with estimations of dates of bruises, etc. In many formats the use of photographs (with written consent) is encouraged.

Section 4 involves an assessment of the elderly person's usual lifestyle, specifically enquiring about medication, ambulation, continence, feeding, hygiene, finances, and family involvement (with ranges from totally independent to totally dependent).

Section 5 is a social assessment identifying interactions between client and family, friends, and other caregivers. It involves detailed knowledge of social support systems and the client's ability to express needs and participate in daily activities (often relying on observational skills). A financial assessment is also made.

Section 6 is the medical assessment, often backed up by

laboratory and radiological test results. It can involve assessment of alcohol/substance abuse, dehydration, fractures, excess medication, etc. (again ranging from definite evidence to no evidence).

Section 7 summarizes the evidence and states whether there is proof of either financial/possession abuse, physical or psychological abuse, or neglect.

Section 8 looks at the outcome, i.e. referral to the elder abuse assessment team (US concept) or to lawyer, police, etc. It also provides for comment and follow-up.

The EAI is proving a useful tool in the US by providing a detailed and standardized assessment of elderly people suspected of being abused/inadequately cared for. The evaluation of such screening instruments (modified for a UK population) is urgently needed.

THE ELDERLY MENTALLY INFIRM

This client group forms one of the most difficult diagnostic, treatment, and research areas in all health care. The label 'dementia' is used so inappropriately in most cases that it should be abandoned. The terms acute and chronic confusion are much more accurate and far less stigmatizing.

Acute confusion

This is the term used to best describe the form of confusion otherwise known as 'delirium'. It can occur over minutes or hours or even have a slower onset, being present for up to 3 months. The person is usually disorientated in time and place and may look unwell, flushed, and even sweating. They are intermittently drowsy and often have visual hallucinations. Speech may be slurred and the person may be unsteady on his or her feet. In young people the stimulus to produce this effect has to be severe, e.g. malaria, meningitis, etc. In the elderly almost any disease state can cause it but characteristically conditions such as urinary-tract infections, pneumonia, heart attacks, and small strokes are the most common causes. Drug side-effects are another common cause of acute confusional states. Once the acute confusion is correctly recognized as an illness (and not as due to old age), a cause has to be found and correct treatment can be given. This may take a period of time but most cases of acute confusion are fully reversible.

Chronic confusion

This is somewhat more complicated in that two subgroups can be identified: reversible and non-reversible (the dementias). Chronic confusion by definition has been present for at least 3 months and usually for a lot longer.

The reversible causes are extremely important as they account for about 10% of cases and if not picked up a mistaken diagnosis of 'dementia' may be made. Conditions such as hypothyroidism (underactivity of the thyroid gland) and syphilis (a venereal disease) can present as a chronic confusional state. Another important condition not to miss is depression – pseudodementia. Some brain tumours are benign and can be removed, e.g. meningioma, and these too can present with chronic confusion.

The irreversible causes are more common and most can be diagnosed from the history. The two most common conditions are Alzheimer's disease and multi-infarct dementia. Alzheimer's disease is a condition of slow onset with a gradual decline in numerous faculties. The most obvious loss is in short-term memory though many other aspects of brain function are affected, e.g. judgement, numeracy skills, personality, etc. The disease can have a slow course but in a few people it appears to be aggressive and the mental decline is accompanied by physical ill health and death occurs within a few years. In multi-infarct dementia the story is one of periodic sharp declines in mental and often physical health associated with the 'minor' strokes. The brain is usually affected in a more haphazard way and yet memory is still a major area of loss of function. The two conditions can prove to be difficult to distinguish in some people, though a CT brain scan may show up the infarcts (areas of furred-up blood vessels resulting in lack of blood and an area of tissue death). Often a definitive diagnosis is only made at post-mortem.

The two conditions account for about 10% of 'dementia' in the over 65s and 20% in the over 80s. To complicate matters those with chronic confusion can develop an infection and so become acutely worse, the so-called acute on chronic confusional state. It is therefore obvious that confusional states in the elderly are potentially difficult areas to make firm diagnoses and predictions. What is clear however is that the word 'dementia' should not be applied until after a vigorous medical history and examination.

It is precisely because of these difficulties that some authorities have developed an assessment process, often called a memory clinic. This usually involves a clinician, a psychiatrist, and a clinical psychologist as its core members although they are usually assisted by nurses, social workers, and therapists. The person is given a thorough medical examination and the psychiatrist assesses for depression and other mental health problems. The clinical psychologist uses various tests to examine the person's memory to see what the deficit is and how severe the impairment. Some clinics have an 'open-access' policy while others receive referrals from GPs and other health care professionals. This system makes sure that all the reversible causes of confusion are looked for and treated if possible.

A client's current mental status should always be ascertained before detailed questions concerning other aspects are obtained. This is to identify the mentally frail/compromised person early, not to dismiss their account of events but to put it into perspective and to allow more time for repetition, etc. No two people with chronic confusion are alike and some objective assessment of their mental state is necessary to try to identify the areas of greatest 'loss'.

One quick screening test is the simple 'mental test score' or abbreviated mental test. This consists of 10 questions which test short- and long-term memory, orientation, and numeracy. It is a rather crude assessment and a low score by itself does not imply a permanent impairment. Its value lies in repetition over time, when a rising score indicates a resolving acute confusion whereas a persistently low score implies a more chronic confusional state. All clients should be told sensitively and politely that it is necessary to test their memory. The clients most upset by testing often have a memory loss that they are aware of and have been trying to cover up. The 10 questions should be written down as most assessors only remember nine!

MENTAL TEST SCORE

Name
Age
Date of birth
Date and time of day
Address
Name of Prime Minister
Date of 1st World War
Place
Remember an address 5 minutes later
Count back from 20 to 1

This assessment may indicate an obvious problem and further history taking must be interpreted with caution. A more detailed evaluation of memory, etc. is provided by performing a 'mini-mental state' test which involves 20 questions [6]. Workers in this area should become conversant with the different aspects of 'confusion' and its assessment. Many clients may need the experienced skills of a memory clinic approach or at least the opinion of a psychogeriatrician.

A poor score on a mental test obviously does not equate with a blanket lack of capacity to consent or mean that a person is totally lacking in judgement concerning certain situations. It is, however, a difficult area where medicine, law, ethics, morality, and professional experience overlap. It is useful to compare the two approaches adopted by the UK and US.

In the UK the balance of assessment is weighted towards professional experience with the sparse legal framework kept in the background. A list of the possible legal aspects that may form part of an individual case can be listed thus:

Mental Health Act 1983
Guardianship
Section 47 of the National Assistance Act (1948)
Court of Protection
Power of Attorney
Enduring Power of Attorney
Agency
The Chronically Sick and Disabled Persons Act
The Living Will (Advance Directive)

All these are expanded upon and discussed in Chapter 5 – Legal issues. The amount of legislation pertaining to the elderly, and the elderly mentally frail especially, is small. This leaves a large 'grey' area of care where professionals are expected to act in the person's 'best interests'. The concepts of competence and judgement are alien to most health care workers who, through lack of legislative guidance, are forced into crude assessment procedures where a statement of whether a person is 'demented' or not forms the basis of a professional decision.

In the US the pendulum has swung the other way with legal issues dominating the field:

Mandatory Reporting Laws (for elder abuse)
Competency hearings
Durable Powers of Attorney (including health care)
The Living Will (Advance Directive)

These issues will also be expanded upon in Chapter 5. However, it is important to note at this stage that there is no major evidence that a State system heavily influenced by governmental process is providing better overall 'care' of its vulnerable elderly [7]. We are convinced that a combination of the two, i.e. professional expertise allowed to assess a situation but backed up by some pertinent legislation, is the correct approach.

The elderly mentally frail need a detailed social and medical assessment process before crisis situations such as suspected abuse or inadequate care occur. In this way valuable time is not used in getting to know the whole picture. The actual episode can be put in some kind of context, which is helpful for the professionals concerned. The degree to which the cognitive impairment (e.g. Alzheimer's disease) affects judgement and consent needs to be assessed and recorded. This may obviously vary for different issues – a person may be considered able to express a wish and decide over some home-care problems, accepting home-help and meals-on-wheels but refusing a day centre; however, he or she may be considered incapable of more complex decisions such as personal payment of bills or cooking at home.

Numerous professionals and carers may be involved in this assessment and ongoing care process. Decisions involving compulsory placement (for whatever reason) are some of the most difficult. Except at times of extreme emergency these decisions should never be rushed. The client's views and wishes are crucial but when circumstances dictate these may have to be overruled. Experience has shown that the more time spent in explaining why a move has to occur the better the long-term outcome. Despite their mental (and often physical) frailty, repeated attempts to reassure, and visits to meet new staff/ carers and see new accommodation can decrease the undoubted morbidity (illness) and mortality (death) associated with moving – the so-called translocation effect [7].

REFERENCES

1. Cochran, C. and Petrose, S. (1987) Elder abuse. The physician's role in identification and prevention. *Illinois Medical Journal*, 171, 241–6.
2. Fulmer, T.T. and O'Malley, T.A. (1987) *Inadequate Care of the Elderly*. Springer Publishing Co., New York.
3. Quinn, M.J. and Tomita, S.K. (1986) *Elder abuse and neglect. Causes, diagnosis and intervention strategies*. Springer Publishing Co., New York.
4. Kosberg, J.I. and Cairl, R.E. (1986) The cost of care index: a case management tool for screening informal care providers. *The Gerontologist*, 26 (3).
5. Fulmer, T.T. (1984) Elder abuse assessment tool. *Dimensions of Critical Care Nursing*, 10 (12), 16–20.
6. Folstein, M.F., Folstein, S.E. and McHugh, P.R. (1975) Minimental method for grading the cognitive state of patients for the clinician. *Journal of Psychiatric Research*, 12, 189–198.
7. Crystal, S. (1986) Social policy and elder abuse. In *Elder Abuse: Conflict in the Family* (ed. Pillemer, K.A. and Wolf, R.S.). Auburn House, Dover, MA.

4

Interventions

Intervention strategies in cases of elder abuse and neglect have consistently caused anxiety and confusion, not least because of a lack of guidelines (see Chapter 6). This is certainly the case in Britain and was the case in America until service providers (health and social) produced policies and procedures followed by legislative changes at state level. The second obstacle that has hindered a service response to elder abuse and neglect has been the conceptual base on which intervention needs to be built. The intervention framework can be either:

- A service response based on the child abuse framework
- A service response based on the spouse abuse framework
- A service response unique to elder abuse.

Many American commentators have suggested that elder abuse has more in common with spouse abuse than child abuse [1, 2]. There is even a debate which suggests elder abuse and neglect should not be defined as a distinct form of abuse and may be classified under the more generic term 'adult abuse', which encompasses all adults 18 years and above. This conceptual framework will influence how different agencies devise their response to elder abuse and neglect. Research to date already suggests that some authorities are either designing their elder abuse policies on the child care model or are happy to follow existing child care procedures [3]. The philosophical basis the authors suggest is used in all circumstances (even in the absence of competence) should be based on a model unique to elder abuse and neglect. This model uses as its core autonomy, empowerment and individual choice. This autonomy for the abused and neglected elderly combines all the freedoms and preference already afforded to adult individuals to choose what, if any, intervention they would wish.

Pillemer [4] suggests that to examine elder abuse with parallels to spouse abuse has certain advantages including seeing:

> Legally independent adults living together out of choice for a variety of emotional and material reasons. The advantage of this comparison is that it does not infantilise the elderly, and emphasises the initiatives they can take on their own behalf.

Any coercive attitude towards the individual because of age or disability would clearly be ageist. However, the problem arises when because of either disability, incompetence (mental health issues), or fear the elderly are victims of abuse/neglect and are in danger of harm by the caregiver. This is an area considered in depth in Chapter 5. The point to be made here is that competent individuals may be in a position of choice not always afforded to incapacitated elders. Every effort should be made with competent elders to pursue a response based on choice, autonomy, and empowerment (Table 4.1).

These two particular models are not mutually exclusive and it should be recognized that the elderly do not fit neatly into the classes of either competent or non-competent individuals. This interface may be the most difficult area to address. Questions concerning choice for elders with cognitive impairment wishing to remain in an abusive situation are complex. The counter-argument is the degree of paternalism the professional is prepared to use in order to protect the elderly. Practitioners may meet situations where the degree of danger to the client outweighs the individual choice to remain in that abusive situation. This will provide a major moral dilemma for the practitioner which he/she alone will have to make. Either to override the person's wishes and remove him/her (if incompetent), or abide by his/her wishes, with all the risks this may involve.

Table 4.1 Case screening

Competent elders		*Non-competent elders*
	Case-screening	
Choice/Freedom		Competence assessment
Advocacy		Global assessment
Empowerment		Case-management
		Legal interventions

However, it is important to suggest that in the main elders can and should where necessary make the decisions that affect their lives.

With the philosophy of choice, autonomy and empowerment to the fore where possible it is necessary to consider what has been learnt so far from elder abuse research interventions. Firstly the research seems to suggest that much abuse has usually been long standing and insidious in its development. Therefore rapid interventions and solutions are often not necessary [4]. The exception will be the case where elders are at serious risk because of changing circumstances – either their own circumstances or those of the carers – and these may include:

- A rapid deterioration in the mental health of either the elder or his/her carer
- A rapid deterioration in the activities of daily living of either the elder or his/her carer

In either of these circumstances swift assessment, both medical and social, is required, followed by intervention. Where there is time to consider options in a multidisciplinary arena safely this can provide a more durable intervention option. Secondly, elders value autonomy above personal safety and comfort [4]. Therefore in situations where danger is not imminent, elders' views should be paramount in decision making. It may be important for the future to also consider the source of the referral. It is also assumed that the front-line agency to provide interventions will firstly be the social services. They may of course refer on if required, and this may be the case if a particular therapeutic intervention is essential, for example Community Psychiatric Nurse intervention. This process could be used for abused or abuser. Social services will also need to refer on if legal interventions are required. Clearly if reports of abuse arrive from the community directly to the social service department a holistic assessment will be completed in the community. If a medical assessment is required the general practitioner could provide assessment at home. This may mean that the client is in close proximity to the abuser who may or may not live with him/her. This is obviously a different situation from a hospital doctor, nurse, or social worker suspecting abuse in a referred patient. There is also the scenario of attenders at day centres and day hospitals showing signs of abuse.

SCREENING

The advent of practice nurses and the 75-years-plus general practitioner screen make it possible to pick up cases of abuse and neglect using screening instruments [5, 6]. A further major component will be the discovery of suspected abuse and neglect in accident and emergency departments [7]. Several screening instruments have been developed for specific use in hospital settings [8–10]. However, there are difficulties; screening instruments should be sensitive (accurate in identifying high-risk subjects) and specific (accurate in correctly exempting low-risk subjects) [11]. To date, the research on elder abuse and neglect remains in a formative stage and risk factors are only now beginning to emerge. It is therefore perhaps premature to assume that screening will pick up large numbers of cases of elder abuse and neglect. What screening will do is alert practitioners to the possibility of abuse which many practitioners are unaware of [8].

These different scenarios, where abuse and neglect may be suspected or discovered, may affect not only the assessment process but also the intervention method (Table 4.2).

The consideration of where the abuse/neglect is discovered will influence the time allowed to frame a response. Individuals who are outside their own homes are usually in a

Table 4.2 Scenarios where abuse and neglect may be suspected or discovered

Discovery or suspicion	
In institutions	*In the community*
Hospital	In the elder's home
Accident and emergency	Screened by GP
Continuing care	Report by community
Day hospital	Report by nurses
Day centre	Report by SW
Respite services	Report by other
Part III	
Residential/nursing care	
Voluntary sector	

position where professionals are considering their health and social status; therefore a multidisciplinary meeting to consider interventions will be necessary, as the regular forum for the particular environment may be insufficient. For elders in their own homes a sharper response may be required. The speed of response will depend on the policy/procedure document for the particular locality.

Interventions generally fall on a continuum from aggressive to passive (Table 4.3).

Table 4.3 Aggressive and passive interventions

Aggressive ← Interventions → Passive	
Police	Advocacy
Bankers	Empowerment
Legal system	Carer support
MHA 1983	Education
Court of protection	Respite care

This particular framework does not encompass all the interventions that may be necessary in elder abuse and neglect, but attempts to show the extreme nature and difficulty of this most complex problem. Between the spectrum of aggressive and passive fall many more interventions. This continuum may also suggest the pace at which the intervention needs to be approached. Aggressive interventions suggest a more dangerous situation for the client than passive interventions. This model also shadows the competing philosophies hypothesis identified by Rosenfield and Newberger [12]. They considered that service professionals approach interventions from a differing theoretical base:

Control model ←——————————→ Compassion model

Control model

Supporters of this model view control and punishment as necessary to alleviate abuse. It is seen in its most potent form with legislation like mandatory reporting laws on elder abuse in the USA. Gelles and Cornell state the position of the control model as follows:

The control approach places full responsibility for actions with the abuser. Control involves removal of the child from the home, arrest of an abusive husband (or wife), and full criminal prosecution of the offender. [13]

This same approach applied to the elder abuse and neglect interventional philosophy would see all abused elders removed from the abuser and all abusers prosecuted. Clearly this drastic type of intervention may only be required in the most severe circumstances. These situations would require not only criminal offences to have taken place but the elder would need to press charges or the police would need to act on their behalf if the elder person is incapable (see Chapter 5, Legal issues). The danger with this process is the reluctance to use what may be considered austere intervention strategies, often when there may be no realistic alternatives.

Compassion model

This model, on the other hand, sees abuse from a non-punitive perspective with no blame attached to the perpetrator. This viewpoint suggests that the abusers are also potentially victims – that in fact they may have acted in this manner because of situations that are made unbearable because of extraneous factors, for example stress and isolation. The model views the abuse from a phenomenological standpoint and seeks to intervene by support and facilitation, with both the abused and abuser. Gelles and Cornell [13] elucidate the dangers of this approach:

- The compassionate clinician may strive to support a family and may actually raise the risk of further violence by relieving the offender of responsibility.
- A clinician's concern for alienating abusive parents or abusive partners may compromise the clinician's judgement and result in the victim being left at risk.
- Should the compassionate approach fail to result in positive change, the human service professional may be left feeling demoralized and burned out [13].

Clearly a balance is necessary, and the two extremes may not always be mutually exclusive. It is possible, as Rosenfield and Newberger suggest, to give compassion and control.

In the best of all possible worlds, the choice of intervention would not boil down to a choice between protecting the child or woman by removal *versus* keeping the family together. The best of all possible worlds would involve appropriate measures of legal control and humane support. [12]

The intervention framework will require consideration alongside the existing knowledge concerning risk factors for elder abuse and neglect. The historical view of the 'stressed carer' requiring support and respite has recently been questioned [14–16]. The suggestion that 'psychopathology' and 'intergenerational transmission of violence' may be high-risk factors for abuse and neglect extends the causative debate. What will become important in the future is the ability to differentiate between different causative factors and intervene appropriately. Stressed caregivers may require support and service provision to reduce stressors. Pathological abusers may need legal interventions. When the competence (mental health status) has been evaluated and the type and potential reason for abuse and neglect considered, an intervention strategy will require formulation. Intervention models are available in the form of a basic matrix design along which service practitioners can follow a path. The first intervention matrix that can be

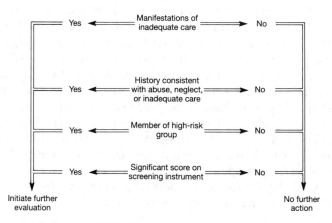

Figure 4.1 Fulmer and O'Malley's matrix.
Used by kind permission of Fulmer, T.T. and O'Malley, T.A. (1987) *Inadequate Care of the Elderly: A Health Care Perspective on Abuse and Neglect*. Springer Publishing Company Inc., New York 10012 [8].

used was designed by Fulmer and O,Malley [8] (Figure 4.1). This matrix considers four separate areas:

- Manifestations of inadequate care (abuse/neglect); for example, injuries, pressure sores, loss of finances.
- History consistent with abuse, neglect or inadequate care; does the history match the explanation given by abused or abuser?
- Member of a high-risk group [17].
- Significant score on a screening instrument [6, 9, 18].

This matrix will require a high degree of flexibility when used as a case-management instrument. This matrix cannot tell whether the elderly have or have not been abused, but it can aid the decision to intervene or not.

Once a decision to intervene has been made or a decision at least to move towards an intervention is considered necessary a further linear matrix will assist the practitioner (Figure 4.2).

It is important to suggest that in certain circumstances even though the decision to intervene is made by a multidisciplinary forum, intervention will not be possible because of the wishes of the elderly victim. However, the practitioner will plan on the assumption that intervention should be possible. Fulmer and O'Malley's intervention matrix starts with the practitioner considering that he/she has discovered an elder with 'unmet needs', which may include abuse and neglect or inadequate care. These needs may require intervention immediately or at some point in the future. If future needs are discovered they will require an in-depth discussion with both the client and carer in order to formulate a future plan with a time schedule, and goals will need to be predetermined with the service agency, the client (if competent), and the carer. The intervention may be of a more urgent nature and the time frame may be critical, usually because of impending harm. If the degree of danger is high, crisis intervention is called for. Fulmer and O'Malley [8] list court, medical, shelter, law enforcement, and other. In Britain interventions include:

Legal interventions (see Chapter 5) including removal of the abuser or abused.
Medical/social interventions (including removal of the abused).

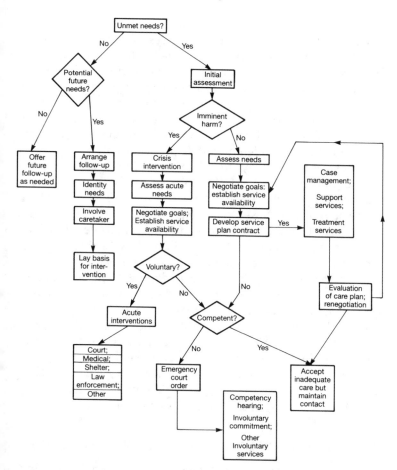

Figure 4.2 Linear matrix when moving towards intervention.
Used by kind permission of Fulmer, T.T. and O'Malley, T.A. (1987)
*Inadequate Care of the Elderly: A Health Care Perspective on Abuse and
Neglect.* Springer Publishing Company Inc., New York 10012 [8].

Shelters (although this is not an option widely available).
Advocacy (also not widely available).

For the willing and competent client empowerment and advocacy to halt the abuse would be the most desirable intervention. This type of service will require development in Britain
because it is mainly available for victims of spouse abuse. This

option of advocacy and empowerment is beginning to become available in America with high degrees of success [19, 20]. If the abused elder does not allow intervention strategies to be employed, the issue of competence will need to be addressed. In the event of a psychiatric assessment suggesting a mental-health problem legal interventions could be used. The most difficult scenario of a competent elder in imminent danger refusing all offers of intervention will return the service practitioner to the moral dilemma previously considered.

Fulmer and O'Malley [8] suggest accepting the inadequate care, but maintaining contact. This may well be the avenue that will need to be followed; however, it can clearly be spelled out to the abuser and abused that contact will be maintained and if at-risk registers are available that names may be placed on them. It is possible that abusers who are aware that they will remain on the service provider's case list may in fact refrain from further abuse. This is particularly important in situations where social isolation of the abused and abuser is apparent. Active social support networks may also deter elder abuse and neglect [4]. There is potential for this type of informal network being provided by the voluntary sector either in the form of informal visits or support groups. For the elderly who are not in imminent danger the exercise is to negotiate goals acceptable to the abused and abuser. Clearly both individuals may require considerable counselling if their views are not compatible.

INTERVENTION STRATEGIES WITH THE COMPETENT ABUSED

Intervention strategies with competent elders should be based if at all possible on a model of advocacy, choice, and empowerment. Advocacy is a relatively new concept in the arena of elderly care, although it has been used for many years for people with learning difficulties. It can be utilized in three differing ways (Table 4.4).

Table 4.4 Advocacy-based intervention strategies

Self-advocacy
Citizen advocacy
Legal advocacy

Self-advocacy

Self-advocacy facilitates the elderly to empower themselves in order to make decisions about their life free from any pressure from other individuals. Victims of elder abuse and neglect may wish to make it evident to the abuser that they wish to live a life free from abuse and neglect. Unfortunately the elderly may feel threatened or intimidated and unable to speak up for themselves. One way forward would be to develop support groups in much the same way that the feminist movement developed them in the 1970s. At a recent conference on the topic of elder abuse and neglect in Tower Hamlets a worker from an emergency shelter spoke of small numbers of elders being part of the small, but consistent, population that seeks refuge from abuse. This advocacy/empowerment model is emerging in America as a front-line intervention strategy. Cabness [19] describes the activities of a shelter for 'abused, neglected, and exploited elderly people' in Washington DC, the aim being primarily to protect; however, it also strives to:

facilitate the recovery of the residents' self esteem and optimum levels of psychosocial functioning.

The shelter uses various strategies, including:

- Supportive counselling (to stimulate informed choice).
- Alcoholics Anonymous support groups (for people with alcohol problems).
- Health promotion (to achieve optimum health).
- Peer interaction (to negate social isolation).
- Transgenerational activities (to stimulate intergenerational interaction).

A similar model is in place in San Antonio, Texas [20] where a 13-bedded shelter is available. The assessment/intervention framework is designed with the following model in mind (Table 4.5).

Gomez [20] stresses the need to consider and address both the trauma caused by the abusive/neglectful situation and residence in a shelter.

The techniques used are similar to the Washington shelter and include:

Table 4.5 Assessment/intervention framework

	Themes
Shelter placement can cause	*Abusive situation can cause*
Loss of control	Expressions of guilt
Self-worth	Anger, fear
Helpessness	Emotional pain, hurt
Sense of safety	Confusion
Frustration	Grief
Anxiety	

- Using unstructured informal yet private dialogue to establish rapport.
- Provide psychological support and explore fears/expectations.
- Attentive listening to facilitate ventilation.
- Promote self-care to reduce sense of helplessness.
- Tap client expertise to reassure self-worth.
- Use life histories in groups to promote self-esteem and socialization.

This type of intervention is clearly more normative than interventions based on removal to residential care. Both of the shelters are of short-stay duration: the Washington shelter has a mean stay of 50 days and San Antonio a maximum 60-day occupancy. This type of short-stay therapeutic option needs consideration within the British context.

Citizen advocacy

The concept of citizen advocacy suggests volunteers or professionals who either provide direct services or represent the interests of the elderly who have been abused/neglected. Critics of citizen advocacy argue that because professionals are attached to organizations (health and social) they can never be truly independent. Certainly the nursing profession sees advocacy as one of its primary roles. *Exercising Accountability* [21] states:

> The code of professional conduct, together with several of its clauses, indicate clearly the expectation that the practitioner

will accept a role as advocate on behalf of his or her patients/clients.

This role may be eminently suitable in cases of elder abuse and neglect. It has been described in situations of spouse abuse where health visitors have been involved. Pahl [22] describes battered women suggesting that before their stay at the refuge health visitors were appreciated for:

... their support, for their acceptance of the woman's own definition of the situation, and for giving relevant and accurate advice and information.

Many community practitioners will find themselves in situations where they will need to advocate and advise on behalf of the elderly who are in an abusive/neglectful situation. Certain cases may be elders who have a history of being involved in domestic abuse over many years and who have graduated into old age without any modification in this behaviour. Homer and Gilleard [16] suggest that:

When this behaviour has been present for many years as an integral part of the relationship it will be very resistant to change.

With situations of graduated abuse and neglect, imposition of intervention strategies will usually be extremely difficult, therefore advocacy and empowerment remain one of the few options for the practitioner.

Legal advocacy

Legal advocacy can be defined as:

Lawyers, and other legally trained individuals who assist persons to exercise or defend their rights.

Legal advocacy may be necessary when the degree of abuse or neglect is sufficient to suggest a highly dangerous situation for the elderly. The legal advocate could work towards a legal position that safeguards the rights of the elder (see Chapter 5). The legal advocate can also intervene when there is any suggestion of financial abuse. When policy/procedure guidelines are being developed legal advisers with particular interests in elderly issues should be co-opted for their particular knowledge and expertise. This will allow health and local authorities to call for legal advice on a regular basis.

INTERVENTION STRATEGIES WITH IMPAIRED ELDERS

Many of the abusive/neglectful situations that professionals will come into contact with will involve the elderly who have some degree of physical/mental impairment (this may also be true of the abuser). Impairment caused by the physical ageing process should not interfere with the choice of intervention, and advocacy and empowerment should be the first-choice intervention. However, impairments affecting the mental health status of the elderly can complicate and confuse the intervention process. The medical assessment process will decide if the elder's mental health status warrants intervention. The choice is then between community interventions (with the danger of perhaps leaving the abused in the care of the abuser) or a residential placement intervention, short term in the first instance, for an assessment period. The least traumatic option should always be considered and some elders consider continued abuse and neglect to be less traumatic than residential care. If community care options are considered an acceptable intervention and assessment of the major areas of difficulty can be made using the 'cost of care index' [6]. Case management should provide a more pluralistic service than the standard interventions of the past including meals-on-wheels, home attendant schemes, volunteers, and respite services both day and night (health and social). Clearly a more comprehensive system will be required in the future in order to provide a more consumer-led service intervention.

INTERVENTION STRATEGIES WITH ABUSERS

Two differing approaches with perpetrators of abuse/neglect are possible and their particular utilization will depend on the impetus behind the abusive/neglectful behaviour:

1. Training in anger and stress management
2. Training in care-giving

Both these interventions can be utilized in situations where the abuse/neglect is either passive or active. They can be applied in situations where the burden of caring is too much [6], or in situations where the carer lacks skills or has inadequate skills. They can also be used when there is a degree of malevolence. Clearly many carers are reluctant carers; they have been expected to take on the caring role without an informed choice and perhaps with little insight into the demands of the caring role. Certainly training in care-giving rarely happens; carers 'pick it up' as they go along. All carers should have the opportunity to make an informed decision as to whether they wish to care or not. If the caring situation becomes burdensome, leading to abuse/neglect, and the carer suggests that they do not have the appropriate caring skills, training sessions could then be utilized. Many community practitioners (district nurses, health visitors, community psychiatric nurses and social workers) already train caregivers in the finer details of care. This type of training is not so far offered in any formal way, certainly not regularly, in Britain. The Americans have produced manuals aimed at both individuals and group leaders [23] to stimulate care-giving skills; similar initiatives are required in Britain. It is important to be aware that many carers consistently face and tolerate various forms of abuse from the elderly person they care for. Sometimes one too many disturbances can tip the balance and generate abuse/neglect that then often leads to institutional interventions. One particular model is described by Scogin *et al.*:

> Care-givers at risk for abuse were offered training through mental health centres on bio-psycho-social issues in aging, problem solving, stress and anger management and utilisation of community resources. [24]

The recipients of the training met for eight weekly sessions in community centres. Although this model was aimed at at-risk carers it could be aimed at abusers and more generally at all potential carers. This is an area that will need further consideration in order that a more pluralistic response to 'caring' and its potential difficulties can be achieved.

INTERVENTION WHEN THE ABUSER HAS MENTAL HEALTH OR ADDICTION PROBLEMS

Professionals sometimes discover family members, who may be carers, suffering from either mental health of addiction problems. The risk that these individuals will abuse or neglect seems to be high [4, 16]. These carers may need evaluation and intervention from a variety of health and social sources, including mental health services, Alcoholics Anonymous and voluntary addiction agencies. The difficulty will arise when the individual does not accept he/she has a problem that requires intervention. Voluntary acceptance of help will enable a smooth and amicable intervention to take place by the professional involved. Unfortunately this agreeable scenario is often difficult to achieve and in cases of dangerous levels of abuse and neglect a more formal approach may be required involving legal intervention. Certainly perpetrators of abuse who refuse voluntary treatment for their addiction may receive probation orders with condition of treatment. The Americans are considering taking this a step further with mandatory education about the ageing process and the caring role as part of an alternative to criminal sanctions. This type of alternative needs evaluation before implementation in Britain. Until alternatives to criminal sanctions have been evaluated it may in fact be necessary to increase the few sanctions that are already in place in Britain. Pillemer suggests that one form of deterrent in family violence is indeed to increase the 'costs' of abusive behaviour. In effect it may be necessary to change the balance so that:

> . . . being arrested . . . would greatly outweigh the rewards obtained from abusive behaviour. [11]

This type of intervention may be a distant idea in the elder abuse debate in Britain; however, it must not be dismissed just because the police have consistently had a low profile in family violence. It may be that this is the point in time when a higher-profile 'legal face' is necessary.

FINANCIAL ABUSE

Financial abuse is probably the most difficult of all the abusive behaviours to both detect and stop. Practitioners regularly suspect that monies and property transactions are taking place either against the wishes of the elderly or even without their prior knowledge. Most practitioners feel inadequately equipped and therefore helpless to intervene. It has previously been suggested that legal advocacy may be necessary, whilst the skills of a legal representative can also be utilized if the practitioner suspects financial misdemeanours. Probably the only way to intervene is when the elderly complain that their financial position is being tampered with. It may be possible for a citizen or legal advocate to help empower an elder to confront a perpetrator of financial abuse. Banks and building societies can be approached on behalf of consenting elders to restrict access to their monies. When case-management is fully enforced it might be possible in a multidisciplinary forum to seek financial advice from the elder's favoured institution. In the market economy of America this is a common scenario. Clearly this is an area where we need to watch the American service intervention and learn accordingly.

It will become increasingly obvious that the standard interventions that were barely adequate in the elderly care arena for the last twenty years will not be sufficient in the next decade. This will be particularly true for the realm of elder abuse and neglect. The public sector budget is being increasingly tightened, therefore 'innovation', 'welfare pluralism', 'case management' and the 'market economy' will need to move from rhetoric towards pragmatic service interventions.

These innovative interventions will also require thorough assessment and evaluation. Bookin and Dunkin sum up the situation:

> Successful intervention in the area of elder abuse will also require the development of new helping techniques, rather than simple transference of skills used in working with other clients with other types of problems. The elderly, frequently left out of case plans utilising family therapy, should be considered as an integral part of treatment. [25]

REFERENCES

1. Crystal, S. (1986) Social policy and elder abuse. In *Elder Abuse: Conflict in the Family* (ed. Pillemer K. and Wolf, R.). Auburn House Publishing Company, Dover, MA.
2. Pillemer, K.A. and Finkelhor, D. (1988) Elder abuse: its relationship to other forms of domestic violence. In *Family Abuse and its Consequences* (ed. Hotaling, G.T.). Sage Publications, Beverly Hills, CA.

3. Kingston, P.A. (1991) Elder abuse. In *Elder Abuse: An Exploratory Study* (ed. McCreadie, C.). Age Concern Institute of Gerontology, King's College London.
4. Pillemer, K.A. (1990) Ten tentative truths about elder abuse. *Journal of Health and Home Rehabilitation of the Adult*, Spring, 465–83.
5. Homer, A. and Kingston, P. (1991) Screening by nurse practitioners could prevent elder abuse. *Care of the Elderly*, May.
6. Kosberg, J.I. and Cairl, R.E. (1986) The cost of care index: a case management tool for screening informal care providers. *The Gerontologist*, 26 (3), 273–8.
7. Kingston, P.A. and Hopwood, A. (In press) The elderly person in the accident and emergency department. In *Issues in Accident and Emergency Care* (ed. Sbaih, L.). Chapman and Hall, London.
8. Fulmer, T.T. and O'Malley, T.A. (1987) *Inadequate Care of the Elderly: A Health Care Perspective on Abuse and Neglect*. Springer Publishing Company, New York.
9. Breckman, R.S. and Adelman, R.D. (1988) *Strategies for Helping Victims of Elder Mistreatment*. Sage Publications, London.
10. Jones, J. *et al.* (1988) Emergency department protocol for the diagnosis and evaluation of geriatric abuse. *Annals of Emergency Medicine*, 17 (10), 1006–15.
11. Pillemer, K.A. and Suitor, J.J. (1990) Prevention of elder abuse. In *Treatment of Family Vilence*, (ed. Ammerman, R.T. and Hersen, M.). John Wiley, New York.
12. Rosenfield, A. and Newberger, E.H. (1977) Compassion *vs* Control: conceptual and practical pitfalls in the broadened definition of child abuse. *Journal of the American Medical Association*, 237, 2086–8.
13. Gelles, R.J. and Cornell, C.P. (1990) *Intimate Violence in Families*. Sage Publications, London.
14. Wolf, R.S., Strugnell, C. and Godkin, M. (1982) *Preliminary Findings from the Three Models Project on Elderly Abuse*. University of Massachusetts, University Center of Aging, Worcester, MA.
15. Pillemer, K.A. and Wolf, R.S. (1986) *Elder Abuse: Conflict in the Family*. Auburn House Publishing, Dover, MA.
16. Homer, A. and Gilleard, C. (1990) Abuse of elderly people by their carers. *British Medical Journal*, 301, 1359–62.
17. Pillemer, K. (1986) Risk factors in elder abuse: results from a case-control study. In *Elder Abuse: Conflict in the Family* (ed. Pillemer, K. and Wolf, R.). Auburn House, Dover, MA.
18. Kosberg, J.I. (1988) Preventing elder abuse: identification of high risk factors prior to placement decisions. *The Gerontologist*, 28 (1), 43–50.
19. Cabness, J. (1989) The emergency shelter: a model for building self esteem of abused elders. *Journal of Elder Abuse and Neglect*, 1 (2), 71–82.
20. Gomez, E. (1991) *Clinical Intervention in an Emergency Shelter for Adult Protective Service Clients*. Paper presented to the Eighth

Annual Adult Protective Services Conference, San Antonio, Texas, USA.

21. *Exercising Accountability: A framework to assist nurses, midwives and health visitors to consider ethical aspects of professional practice.* (1989) UKCC.

22. Pahl, J. (1982) Men who assault their wives: What can health visitors do to help? *Health Visitor*, 55 (10), 528–31.

23. Mahoney, D.F., Shippee-Rice, R. and Pillemer, K.A. (1988) *Training Family Care-givers: A Manual for Group Leaders.* Nursing Department and the Family Research Laboratory of the University of New Hampshire.

24. Scogin, F. *et al.* (1989) Training for abusive care-givers: an unconventional approach to an intervention dilemma. *Journal of Elder Abuse and Neglect*, 1 (4), 73–86.

25. Bookin, D. and Dunkin, R.E. (1985) Elder abuse issues for the practitioner. *Social Casework*, 66, 3–12.

5

Legal issues

As adults elderly people theoretically have full access to all the legal services available to other adult members of society (following crimes of violence, theft, etc.). The situation can be clear cut with a lucid elderly victim preferring charges, backed up by witnesses, with the police and judiciary comfortable in their respective roles. In many cases of elder abuse/inadequate care, however, there is a mentally frail victim, no eye-witnesses to violence, intimidation, or fraud and a manipulating and calculatingly devious abuser. In these situations the police and legal professionals are far from happy with any role offered to them, and even advice may be hard to obtain. Relatives, friends, and statutory and non-statutory services are usually left trying to manage these difficult situations using the few pieces of possibly pertinent legislation available (Table 5.1).

If an obvious crime has been committed, it is important that the victim be encouraged to report the matter to the police. Acts of gross violence and theft currently fit into the usual workload of police departments and hopefully will be dealt with appropriately with a degree of consideration and concern for the victim's age. Reporting a crime is only the beginning of the matter, however; statements have to be taken and court appearances may be necessary – a difficult ordeal at any age.

One early and important issue is the mental competence of the victim. A crime is a crime whatever the competence of the victim, but obviously a poor memory, little recall later, and no witnesses would make a conviction without a confession very difficult. There are no precise definitions for deciding when a person is no longer capable of making valid decisions for themselves. In the UK it is a very imprecise and grey area usually decided upon by doctors making a personal judgement following a full history and examination (hopefully on more than

Table 5.1 Possible available legislation

Mental Health Act 1983
Guardianship
Section 47 of the National Assistance Act
(1948)
Court of Protection
Power of Attorney
Enduring Power of Attorney
Agency
The Chronically Sick and Disabled Persons Act
The Living Will (Advance Directive)*
Wills

*Has no current legal standing in the UK.

one occasion). The point of the history and examination is to rule out acute/subacute confusional states or a depressive illness which may recover. It also assesses the cognitive state (orientation in time, place, and person, reasoning ability, speech, writing, and calculation). A physician in health care of the elderly, a psychiatrist or psychologist may individually or as a team assess a patient. Professional judgements may vary but more importantly a person's competency will vary depending on the issue being assessed. A person may not be able to calculate, remember addresses, or reason an argument but they may give valid answers to certain questions and to a limited extent indicate preferences (where they would like to live and with whom). The issues around mental competency are complex and need greater evaluation with professionals (both medical and legal). In the US mental competence is a legal matter and is hence viewed differently.

If a person is deemed incompetent, i.e. no longer capable of managing any of his/her affairs, then the courts must appoint someone into that caring supervisory role. The Law Society here referred the matter of decision making and mental incapacity to the Law Commission in 1990 and the subject was included in the programme for law reform. The current inadequate situation has been acknowledged and hopefully the Law Commission will address such issues as emergency powers for crisis intervention, consent to medical treatment, financial management, and specifically protection from abuse. Currently, however, health care professionals must continue to walk the tightrope between acting in the best interests of the patient, i.e. the common law 'duty of care', and of infringing a person's individual freedoms and rights.

An obscure and little-known legal case in 1907 involved an elderly woman affected by strokes who was being assaulted by her neice. The court felt that a great-nephew could institute proceedings on behalf of the victim because '. . . if the person assaulted is so feeble, old and infirm as to be incapable of instituting proceedings, and is not a free agent but under the control of the person committing the assault, the information may be laid by a third person'. [1] The authors thus feel that the police could initiate action on the client's behalf and prosecute most cases of even minor assault. [1]

MENTAL HEALTH ACT 1983

The Mental Health Act [2] is based upon a common law principle: the duty that we all have to help someone who appears to be unable to make an appropriate judgement of their own needs for care. Often attempts are made using the Mental Health Act to admit a person to an institution against his or her will. However, the Act was not intended to be used for patients with organic brain disease – dementia is not classed as a treatable mental illness for the purposes of the Act. However, in practice there are sections of the Act that can be useful in a commonsense management approach (Table 5.2).

Section 136 is intended to be used by the police if they find someone whom they suspect is mentally ill and in need of assessment. It allows for the person to be taken to a suitable place, usually a hospital, for up to 72 hours. Section 4 is also used for emergency admissions for 72 hours but requires a relative or social worker and a doctor to make a recommendation. As dementia (chronic confusion) is not classed as a treatable mental illness it cannot be good practice to use these sections of the Mental Health Act to gain admission.

Many people with chronic confusion (dementia) in hospital, local authority residential care or in the private sector have never formally consented to be there and are, in effect, held under *de facto* detention [3]. Only compulsorily detained people have any formal protection of their rights. This situation has been partially resolved in Scotland with legislation stem-

Table 5.2 The Mental Health Act

Section 2. Admission for assessment and treatment for up to 28 days. A relative or a social worker together with two doctors (GP plus a psychiatrist usually) must make the recommendation.

Section 3. Admission for treatment for up to 6 months. A relative and social worker must agree that treatment is necessary and the same medical recommendations pertain as in Section 2.

Section 4. Emergency admission for up to 72 hours. A relative or social worker together with one doctor (usually GP) must make the recommendation.

Section 5 (2). Allows a patient already receiving treatment in hospital to be kept for up to 72 hours. Recommendation made by the hospital doctor.

Section 5 (4). Allows a patient already receiving treatment in hospital to be kept for up to 6 hours until a doctor can be found. Recommendation usually made by the ward nurse.

Section 136. Allows a police constable to remove a person presumed to have mental illness from a public place to a place of safety for up to 72 hours.

Section 135 also contains a 'place of safety' provision.

ming from the independently constituted Scottish Mental Welfare Commission which offers 'extensive protective functions in respect of persons who may be, by reason of mental disorder, incapable of adequately protecting their person or their interests'.

GUARDIANSHIP

The Mental Health Act 1983 permits local authority social service departments to provide guardianship to persons suffering from a 'mental disorder' as a way of protecting vulnerable people and as a means of ensuring that a responsible person is empowered to make major decisions for them [4]. In a review of guardianship orders in one area the majority were used in elderly people with dementia, the most common reason for its use being to place the person in residential care [5]. The guardian has three main powers. Firstly he or she can require the patient to live at a specified place. Secondly the patient can be required to attend specified places at specified times for medical treatment, e.g. day hospital or day centre. Thirdly the guardian can require access to be given to a doctor, approved social worker, or other specified person [6]. The application for the order is very similar to that for a compulsory admission under the Mental Health Act, i.e. a close relative or social worker on the recommendation of two doctors. A guardianship order lasts 6 months but can be renewed. A guardian has no access to the person's money or household goods.

In many districts social workers and doctors have very little experience of guardianship orders and hence are reluctant to use them. In addition they impose a responsibility on social services (via a named person), not a welcome management arrangement. Many districts do not consider dementia to be a mental disorder and hence abrogate their responsibility that way. In some cases of abuse/inadequate care where the victim has a mental disorder (including dementia) a guardianship order may be a valuable and useful tool and its use should not be denied to people because of departmental 'policies'. It is hoped that a more flexible and useful version will be forthcoming.

SECTION 47 OF THE NATIONAL ASSISTANCE ACT (1948)

This is sometimes used to place a person in hospital or care compulsorily against his/her will. It relates to people deemed unable to care for themselves and not receiving (usually refusing) care at home. The person has to suffer from a 'grave chronic disease' (no definition in the Act) or be aged, infirm, or physically incapacitated and be living in unsanitary conditions. The Act is not clear in stating if both conditions (lack of care and chronic disease/infirmity) have to apply. The local community physician acting with the local authority applies to a magistrate's court for an order committing the person to institutional care (usually either a local hospital or old people's home). Its use is declining because of the obvious lack of safeguarding of human rights and personal autonomy. In the past it has been used to remove 'difficult' people. It is still contemplated as a last-resort measure when dealing with cases of gross personal neglect in the absence of mental illness and where the person is adamantly refusing all forms of help yet is obviously failing and living in increasing squalor.

COURT OF PROTECTION

The Court of Protection is a branch of the Lord Chancellor's department. The Court appoints a 'receiver' to act on behalf of a person who can no longer manage his or her finances. The application procedure is lengthy and expensive. Where there are only limited resources the Court can simply permit assets to be converted to cash (to pay bills). The use of the Court should be contemplated by relatives or carers of persons (especially those with dementia) who cannot manage their financial affairs. It acts as protection against future allegations of misbehaviour. In cases of established concern there may be a distinct conflict of interests and the Court can be asked to appoint an unbiased receiver.

The Lord Chancellor's office also has visitors to help with particular problems. The medical visitors are consultant psychiatrists to help with difficult decisions on whether a person can manage or make a will, etc. General visitors will call in on clients in various settings and the visitors from the Management Division make a yearly visit to those clients for whom the Division is acting as receiver (where no other person can be found to do so).

POWER OF ATTORNEY

This allows an appointed person (called an attorney or appointee) to act for another on his or her behalf (usually on financial matters but it can be limited to other particular topics). The document is straightforward and only has to be signed and witnessed. This is often done by a solicitor who has not seen the person (or assessed their competence). This is important because a Power of Attorney cannot be used if the person is mentally incapable of understanding its implications, and becomes invalid if that person becomes incapable. In these circumstances it must be replaced by a Court of Protection application.

ENDURING POWER OF ATTORNEY

An Enduring Power of Attorney means that an attorney (appointee) can continue to manage the affairs of someone who later becomes incompetent. The attorney (appointee) simply registers the enactment of the enduring powers with the Court of Protection when the time comes. If health care professionals suspect abuse of the enduring Power of Attorney (i.e. not acting in the client's best interests) then at some stage representation should be made to the attorney. It is possible to appoint more than one person as an attorney and this may act as a safeguard. If worries continue, they should be reported to the Court of Protection.

AGENCY

A nominated person (the Agent) acts on behalf of a frail person within specified instructions. This is most often seen in the social security system where a pensioner will nominate someone to collect his/her benefits from the Post Office. The Agent can only collect the money and must then hand it to the person concerned. Many people use this form of help to enable friends, neighbours, or home helps to collect pensions. There is a set procedure for this form of transaction. The pensioner deletes 'I acknowledge receipt of the above sum' which is printed on the pension. They then sign it as usual and write and sign on the back:

'I am unable to go to the Post Office and I authorise (signature)'. This must be witnessed by someone other than the Agent. The Agent also has to sign the following:

'I am today the authorised agent. I certify that the payee is alive today. I acknowledge receipt of the amount shown overleaf which I will pay to the payee forthwith (signature)'.

DISABLED PERSONS ACT 1986

This Act was passed by Parliament in 1986, but its 18 sections are being brought into force gradually. The Act gives disabled people four rights:

The right to representation – in cases of mental or severe physical incapacity the local authority can appoint a representative on behalf of the disabled person or ask a voluntary organization to appoint someone.

The right to assessment – this includes any disabled person who asks for services from the local authority under Section 2 of the Chronically Sick and Disabled Persons Act 1970.

The right to information – if a disabled person receives a service from social services then they must also be informed of the other services available and any other relevant services provided by other local authorities.

The right to consultation – the Chronically Sick and Disabled Persons Act 1970 states that certain councils and committees should have a disabled person or someone with special knowledge on that committee. The 1986 Act states that the person can only be appointed after consultation with organizations of disabled people [7].

LIVING WILLS

Mentally competent individuals can refuse protracted health care if they so wish – regardless of its ultimate effect on their health. Doctors and some other health care professionals dealing with the mentally incompetent are governed by what is known as 'good medical practice'. As the person concerned cannot give consent measures are taken 'in their best interest'. Hopefully most teams of professionals dealing with such issues in an elderly patient in the UK would discuss the dilemma with the person's relatives or carers, although they have no legal force to influence the doctors one way or the other (Enduring Powers of Attorney specifically exclude medical matters). 'Good medical practice' may mean that on some occasions a person undergoes an operation or is given some form of treatment that the relatives or carers know would have been refused had the person been mentally competent.

In the United States there is legislation to insist on the personal autonomy of the person under consideration being paramount. To ensure this the person must sign a statement basically saying how far he/she would like the doctors to go in the event of him/her becoming incapable of giving informed consent and developing a life-threatening illness. Obviously this procedure must be done before any brain damage has occurred.

This statement is called a Living Will (generically called an Advance Directive) and describes a form of anticipated consent [8]. In addition to the Living Will an enduring power of attorney (for health care) allows the competent person to appoint an advocate to act on his/her behalf and act as the 'fine tuning' to the whole mechanism. The belief is that the Living Will returns autonomy to an otherwise disenfranchised adult and is a departure from a very paternalistic area of medicine. Such a document has no legal validity in the UK.

Views in this area run along a spectrum – from the concept of it being morally wrong, through the premise that good medical practice already allows people to die in certain circumstances, to the notion that this form of legislation (if adopted) falls short of the ultimate upholding of autonomy and dignity, that is the right to die at a time of one's own choosing (i.e. euthanasia). Living Wills are usually in a prescribed form of declaration, but can vary as to complexity. An example is given below.

1. If the time comes when I am incapacitated to the point when I can no longer actively take part in decisions for my own life, and am unable to direct my physician as to my own medical care, I request that I be allowed to die and not be kept alive through life-sustaining measures if my condition is deemed irreversible. I do not intend any direct taking of my life, but only that my dying not be unreasonably prolonged.

2. It is my express wish that if I should develop
   (a) Brain disease of severe degree, or
   (b) Serious brain damage resulting from accidental or other injury or illness, or
   (c) Advanced malignant disease, in which I would be unable or mentally incompetent to express my own opinion about accepting or declining treatment;
   and if two independent physicians conclude that, to the best of current medical knowledge, my condition is irreversible, then I request that the following points (3)–(6) be taken into consideration.

3. Any separate illness (e.g. pneumonia, or a cardiac or kidney condition) which may threaten my life should not be given active treatment unless it appears to be causing me undue physical suffering. Cardiopulmonary resuscitation should not be used if the existing quality of my life is already seriously impaired.

4. In the course of such an advanced illness, if I should be unable to take food, fluid, or medication, I would wish that

these should not be given by any artificial means, except for the relief of obvious suffering.

5. If, during any such illness, my condition deteriorates and, as a result, my behaviour becomes violent, noisy, or in any other way degrading, or if I appear to be suffering severe pain, any symptom should be controlled immediately by appropriate drug treatment, regardless of the consequences upon my physical health and survival, to the extent allowed by law.

6. The object of this declaration is to minimize distress or indignity which I may suffer or create during an incurable illness, and to spare my medical advisers and/or relatives the burden of making difficult decisions on my behalf.

It is often stated that the United States is a more legalistic society than the UK. There is high status and pay for members of the legal profession and they are seen as constantly expanding a dynamic written constitution. This viewpoint is epitomized in the field of elder abuse where in the 1980s all States passed some laws relating to the topic. At first glance there appears to be some uniformity relating to the laws but this is misleading. Each of the 50 States uses its own definition of elder abuse and these vary widely, making the same act of violence abuse in one State but not in another. As Wolf puts it:

This lack of uniformity has hindered efforts to determine the scope of the problem and to build the knowledge base necessary for development of intervention and preventive programs. [9]

Although the States vary in their governing statutes and regulations, some important agencies and laws can be recognized for their potential modification to a UK setting. For those interested, a full glossary of American terminology related to elder abuse is available in Douglass' publication [10]. In the US there are Agencies on Aging – local, area, or State. These are governmental agencies designated in the Older Americans Act of the United States Congress to co-ordinate the delivery of services at the local level and supported by Federal funds. An Area Agency on Aging usually comprises a city, county, or group of counties whose respective agencies serve as information and referral sources for families seeking assistance with the care of an ageing family member, or for an ageing citizen on his or her own behalf.

The American system of criminal justice is a network of police agencies, courts, and correctional institutions with varying degrees of autonomy and interdependency, acting toward the common purposes of prevention and control of crime. This system does not make laws but upholds them, and has three primary sections: enforcement, adjudication, and correction. The concept of Guardian features prominantly in US law [10]. A guardian is a person or agency appointed by the court who is given authority to control, manage, and protect a person and his or her financial and property assets. A guardian can be given wide authority over finances, investments and accommodation, and be made responsible in cases of mental incompetence (if no one is willing to be power of attorney). The guardian can be a relative or friend or a total stranger (usually then an attorney appointed by the court). There are other forms of guardian. Guardian Ad Litem is a special guardian appointed by the court to represent the interests of an incompetent individual in litigation cases. The court can appoint a limited guardian where a person is incompetent only in certain aspects of life (e.g. finances). The guardian has powers to act only in the client's area of incompetence. A public guardian is appointed by the court (an officer of the court) and acts as guardian for many incompetent clients. A plenary guardian is a person or agency appointed by the court to have complete control over an incompetent person's entire affairs.

Adult Protective Services (APS) is a public or non-profit-making service that acts on the suspicion or a report of personal harm and is State funded. The report may come from the individual concerned, a neighbour, a statutory or professional source, or another agency. It is their role to gather evidence and determine if adults are at risk of personal injury, harm, or less directly due to actions or inactions of others or to the personal inability to care for themselves or their property. Protective service agencies generally undertake case management or referral until the charges are verified and resolved to the advantage of the individual or dismissed as invalid. There exists at the present time considerable debate over current US legislation regarding the prevention of elder abuse. After a flurry of activity at the federal level between 1978 and 1981 (culminating in a Congressional Select Committee report: 'Elder Abuse: An Examination of a Hidden Problem'), expectations were raised that the federal government would quickly enact a comprehensive legislative measure similar to child abuse legislation. This would provide resources to the States specifically for elder abuse prevention programmes.

Although federal support for APS exists under Social Security legislation, it is noted that little progress has been made during the past decade in achieving this goal of ring-fenced federal funding through legislation. The present situation is that a bill entitled 'The Prevention, Identification and Treatment of Elder Abuse' is making its slow passage through Congressional hearings. If the Bill becomes law its primary aim will be to provide financial assistance to elder abuse prevention, treatment, and identification programmes through the establishment of a National Center on Elder Abuse in the Department of Health and Human Services, a federal body. This agency (APS) appears to be the most likely structure to be transferable across the Atlantic. Personal observation shows it to work in a similar way to a branch of our Social Services. However, this means a move away from the generic pattern currently established but this is hardly insurmountable as the separate sections set up for children and clients with learning difficulties have shown. Case management has to be in place by 1993 and a section of elderly services with an expertise in elder abuse/ inadequate care within a district social service structure would have a lot to commend it, especially if protective legislation is enacted. This would not only force local authorities to allocate cases but ensure that this particularly vulnerable client group received the help of qualified, indeed highly qualified, staff.

Almost every State has put into place mandatory reporting laws requiring any person who has reasonable cause to believe that an elderly person is being abused, neglected, or exploited to report his or her concerns to the Adult Protective Services (APS). This team, for the most part qualified social workers, in turn investigates and assesses each referral, filing a report for the Attorney-General if criminality is a feature. The efficacy of mandatory reporting has, however, recently come under serious criticism, not least by APS workers themselves. It is often referred to as 'mandatory dumping', emphasizing the concern that agencies were often perceived to be exonerating themselves from responsibility in dealing with elder abuse referrals by 'passing the buck' to the APS.

The mandatory reporting issue also comes under heavy criticism for its implied effectiveness in preventing elder abuse. APS workers consistently point to the unreal expectations placed upon them to produce 'acceptable' results, even where these may be against the wishes of the service users. The point is also made that mandatory reporting can impinge upon the elderly person's right to autonomy by effectively removing their control of the situation [11]. The general feeling appears to be that the system of mandatory reporting, although well intentioned, has been hastily implemented and may in fact contribute little to the prevention of elder abuse.

Outlining these issues, the President of the National Committee for the Prevention of Elder Abuse, Rosalie Wolf, stressed that the mandatory reporting systems of various States should be measured for their effectiveness in elder abuse prevention.

The concept of the Living Will/Advance Directive was developed in the US possibly as a direct result of the overt poor clinical practice forced on the medical profession by the legalistic nature of American society. Dissenters in the debate in the UK feel that good clinical practice already allows for appropriate care of the mentally incompetent and that legislation is not needed. Pro Advance Directives see them as an advance against medical paternalism, and that regardless of the level of 'good practice' some degree of personal autonomy should enter into these vital decision areas. All States in the US now have Living Will/Advance Directive laws allowing cessation of treatment to the terminally ill in certain circumstances. The frontiers of this ethically and morally difficult subject are constantly being pushed forwards. In 1991 a referendum in the State of Washington narrowly lost the vote on whether to extend the rights of the patient to include euthanasia – the deliberate taking of life [12].

These issues still have to be thoroughly debated in the UK. Age Concern opened up the argument with its publication on Living Wills, openly advocating a legally enforceable version with an enduring power of attorney for health issues (to act as the fine-tuning mechanism) [8]. As a co-author I was aware of a lot of interest at the time especially amongst elderly people via 'phone-ins' and debates. There was a consistent majority in favour of such a system. Age Concern also advocate a Charter of Rights for elderly people, further legally empowering them in certain circumstances:

That a general power be introduced enabling local authorities
  (a) to promote the welfare of elderly people, and
  (b) advise/guide and assist old people and to make available resources as necessary.

That a specific duty on local authorities be introduced to consider the care of individual vulnerable old people.

That an intervention Order be introduced to enable individual old people and/or carers to oppose or to appeal against a decision of the local authority and to enable a local authority to oppose or appeal against the decision of an individual.

The above legislation to be backed up by limited Emergency Powers [7].

Comparison is often made with the legal framework surrounding the issue of child abuse. Direct comparisons are fraught with dangers and indeed the differences outnumber the similarities [P. Riley, unpublished communication]. In child abuse strong influences include the large body of UK research, agreed definitions, and a strong legal framework – all missing in elder abuse. In addition, because of these strong influences Social Service departments (with Government encouragement) have ensured high levels of qualified staff in Child Care services and a good range of knowledge at senior management level. Contrast these last points in their dealings with the elderly where, because there is no legislation, the elderly are often not even allocated a staff member, being seen as low priority. If allocated there is a preponderance of unqualified staff in elderly services, compounded by a poor, often non-existent, knowledge of the issue of elder abuse/inadequate care at a senior management level.

People dealing with suspected cases of elder abuse/ inadequate care often report that the help available from the police is minimal. Unless an obvious crime has been committed or someone is willing to 'take a chance' and accuse an abuser 'on spec', then police disinterest is apparent. This situation must change nationally, and is changing via local initiatives.

Increasing numbers of Family Violence units are being established to develop a police expertise and act as a source of
referral for child abuse and cases of family violence. They
would also seem the obvious choice to become centres of
advice for professionals dealing with suspected elder abuse
cases wanting to 'know the law' and agree on a suitable process for proceding with a case without the danger of an 'all
or none response'. Individuals or groups within Family Violence units should be identified and asked to join local Steering Committees, which are either developing elder abuse/
inadequate care guidelines or modifying those already in existence. This sort of contact is vital to ensure good working
practices aimed at safeguarding the client, the possible abuser,
and the person initiating the enquiry.

Legislation concerning the elderly mentally frail is on the
agenda for change. Legislation concerning elder abuse will
come. Existing good practice should utilize multidisciplinary
steering committees to establish district guidelines, ensuring
ongoing review and modification. In this way the US legislative
excesses should be avoided.

REFERENCES

1. Pivering *v.* Willoughby (1907) 2 KB 296 p. 305. In *The Law and
   Elderly People* (ed. Griffiths, A., Grimes, R.H. and Roberts, G.).
   Routledge, 1990.
2. Department of Health and Welsh Office. (1990) *Code of Practice.
   Mental Health Act 1983.* HMSO, London, 42–6.
3. McWilliam, C. (1991) Senile dementia and the Mental Health Act.
   Care of the Elderly, July, 315–16.
4. Bluglass, R. (1983) Compulsory powers in the community – a
   guardianship. *A Guide to the Mental Health Act.* Churchill Living-
   stone, Edinburgh, 28–31.
5. Wattis, J.P. *et al.* (1990) Use of guardianship under the 1983
   Mental Health Act. *Medicine, Science and the Law*, 30, 313–16.
6. Benbow, S.M. and Germany, E. (1991) Guardianship Orders:
   Underused and undervalued. *Care of the Elderly*, September, 3 (8),
   351–2.
7. Age Concern. (1986) *The Law and Vulnerable Elderly People* (ed.
   Greengross, S.). Grosvenor Press, Portsmouth.
8. Age Concern. (1988) Living wills: consent to treatment at the end
   of life. *Age Concern Working Party Report.* Edward Arnold, London.
9. Wolf, R.S. (1988) Elder abuse: ten years later. *Journal of the
   American Geriatrics Society*, August, 36 (8), 758–62.

10. Douglass, R.L. (1989) *Domestic mistreatment of the elderly – towards prevention*. American Association of Retired Persons. Criminal Justice Services Program Dept., Washington DC, USA.
11. Crystal, S. (1986) Social policy and elder abuse. In *Elder Abuse: Conflict in the Family* (ed. Pillemer, K.A. and Wolf, R.S.). Auburn House, Dover, MA.
12. *British Medical Journal* (1991) 303 (16 November), 1223.

6

Health authority and social service co-operation

The question of how Health and Social Services can best work together in order to produce a comprehensive system aimed at prevention, assessment, and intervention needs addressing. The traditional view is that health and social services have difficulty understanding each other's interventional philosophy. There are indications that a more positive trend towards joint planning is now taking place. However, difficulties remain and a learning process from previous experiences with child abuse and spouse abuse will be necessary to take full advantage of the successes and failures from these experiences. The lessons from America will also prove invaluable when a response to elder abuse is beginning to be framed in Britain. The position to date would suggest that there is a rapid movement by both social service departments and health authorities to produce guidelines on elder abuse and neglect. Research by Hildrew [1] suggests that 11 social service departments in England and Wales had guidelines by the summer of 1991, with another 25 authorities well advanced in their plans. A 1992 survey [2] of all social services/social work departments received a 75% response rate with the following findings:

- 75% of the replying departments reported that they either had procedures (15%); had procedures in draft form (30%), or had working parties actively considering these issues (30%).
- Of the responses in group A (guidelines/procedures fully implemented) and group B (guidelines/procedures in draft form), 58% had or were working on a multiagency basis with health and police departments.

- 20% had or were intending to have 'at-risk registers' (some authorities considered using other titles).
- Equal opportunities, advocacy, and staff support systems were given priority.

This shows a positive trend in the last two years to produce policies and procedures. However, there are still difficulties, especially with the changing reorganizational structure of health services and social services. Research in 1990 [3] found that within health districts individual departments were not aware of each other's work. In a research reply one district mental health service stated:

We have recently addressed the need for a clear policy/procedure relating to abuse of the elderly.

The Elderly care unit within the same health district replied suggesting their procedure included a case conference and respite if requested. They then went on to request:

If you have any replies where formal procedure and policies are adhered to, I would be most grateful if you could let me know.

This problem of different sectors/units within a district service writing policies in isolation needs careful consideration at district health authority level. It became apparent that several health authorities were working on the formulation of either working parties or discussion groups, but that differing departments within the district were working separately. In effect within these districts there was an absence of multidisciplinary co-operation on policy/procedure production. Clearly the present climate of health policy evolution may exacerbate an already complex problem. The scenario of acute services in a District Health Authority with 'Trust' status and the community and mental health services remaining in their present form may not bode well for interdepartment communication. However, not only must all interdistrict departments communicate, the district must also then communicate with the local social service departments. Once again, geographical differences sometimes complicate this communication process. Within the geographical boundaries of certain local authorities are found more than one health district. In these circumstances the communication process will be complex.

Although the future for collaborative and multidisciplinary working is fraught with problems the template that will be suggested has worked successfully in Tower Hamlets. The communication process was helped by the health and social service districts being coterminous. The procedure required to produce such guidelines will differ between local authorities and health authorities, in the main hopefully to satisfy individual geographical, social, cultural, and health requirements. The Tower Hamlets guidelines began with the formation of a multidisciplinary team/working party in the summer of 1990.

The team comprised:

Consultant in health care of the elderly
Consultant psychiatrist in old age
Nurse representative
General practitioner
Social work manager (Hospital)
Social work manager (Community)
Police representative
Voluntary sector representatives
Equal opportunities officer
Community physician
Joint development officer

Draft guidelines were compiled, based upon procedures already in existence in several other local authorities. Once drawn up a draft document was circulated for consultation to all relevant agencies. This should include a large number of other parties:

CONSULTATIVE AGENCIES
Health district agencies
Acute units
Mental health units
Community units
Physiotherapy
Occupational therapy
Trusts
Local authority agencies
All departments

All agencies involved in contractual work
Family health service authorities
General practitioners
Ethnic minority groups
Legal representative
Banks/building societies
Voluntary groups

One extremely useful development that arose from the Tower Hamlets initiative was the post of research and development officer. This developmental post will run for a two-year term and incorporate research into elder abuse and also oversee the implementation of the joint Health and Local Authority guidelines. Other initiatives that have been suggested include the development of nursing positions that address the phenomenon of elder abuse/inadequate care in much the same way that nurses work in the child abuse area.

TOWER HAMLETS LOCAL AUTHORITY AND HEALTH AUTHORITY JOINT ELDER ABUSE/INADEQUATE CARE POLICY GUIDELINES

The guidelines will be partially replicated within this chapter to enable other agencies and individuals to analyse their content, which may stimulate potential ideas for local policy/procedure development. Occasionally a rationale will appear beneath the procedural note.

The Tower Hamlets guidelines start with a rationale for the guidelines and a brief introduction frames the problem of elder abuse and neglect, which includes:

- A definition by Eastman [4]
- Eight 'classic' definitions
- A discussion on widening the definition to 'inadequate care'
- Characteristics of the victim
- Factors associated with abuse/inadequate care
- Recognition
- Theories of causation
- Key references

The main body of the policy follows.

Initial referral

1.1   The aim is that every reported incident of abuse/ inadequate care of an elderly person be treated with the same urgency as that accorded to incidents of child abuse by the duty officer of the relevant neighbourhood or the hospital social work manager.

> *This is a crucial first statement. Child abuse intervention is mandated by law, therefore interventions on the whole are rapid. The aim is to raise elder abuse in importance to that of child abuse.*

1.2   The following information should be obtained on receipt of a referral of suspected abuse/inadequate care of the elderly person.

1.2.1   Elderly person's name, address, telephone number, age, gender, and ethnic background (with language spoken).

1.2.2   Elderly person's close relatives and friends and their telephone numbers, relevant contacts from other agencies and their telephone numbers.

1.2.3   Alleged abuser's name, address, and telephone number, physical description and knowledge of his/her behaviour, relationship to the elderly person, and length of relationship if known.

1.2.4   Description of alleged abuse/neglect/inadequate care, distinguishing clearly between what is reported and what there is current evidence for. Suspicions and evidence obtained to date. (Date of prior contacts, action taken, and by whom are very helpful.)

Rationale
A clear differentiation between fact and speculation must be made; individuals can often speculate about what they think has happened.

1.2.5   General practitioner's name and telephone number, and names and contact numbers for other relevant professionals involved.

1.2.6   Referrer's name and contact number. Description of referrer's involvement in the case to date and how long referrer has known elderly person. (Referrers in some circumstances wish to remain anonymous, but referrals will nonetheless be investigated.)

All referrers giving their names should be notified at the time of referral that their evidence may be needed if they have reported a crime.

Investigation

2.1 The investigation should be carried out by the duty or allocated social worker as soon as possible (within the same time scale as child abuse procedures).

Rationale
It is important that time scales are entered in the policy/ procedure, especially because child abuse legislation is mandated and therefore takes precedence.

2.2 Check with other agencies as to whether the elderly person or alleged abuse is known and under what circumstances.

2.3 Check the department's own records, including the child protection register.

Rationale
Intergenerational transmission of violence is a known risk factor.

2.4 Visit accompanied by another worker if circumstances indicate that such precautions are appropriate.

Rationale
Health and social service workers are at risk in cases of domestic violence [5].

2.5 Interview the dependent elderly person alone without the caregiver and in circumstances in which the elderly person is certain of privacy.

Rationale
This may be extremely difficult in certain circumstances. Should the carer refuse to cooperate, questions need to be asked about why he/she refused to co-operate.

2.6 Explain to the caregiver that he/she will be interviewed separately after the elderly person has been interviewed and that this is normal departmental practice.

2.7 Make a preliminary assessment of the mental capacity of the dependent elderly person.

Rationale
Use of a Mini Mental State Examination is required.

2.8   Pay special attention to suspicious signs and symptoms and the known precipitating factors for abuse/inadequate care.

2.9   Work assessment questions into a conversation in a relaxed manner and not rush the elderly person or the caregiver while being interviewed. (If the interpreting services are required, care must be taken to ensure that the interpreter is someone independent of the elderly person's family and recognized as competent to fulfil this role.)

Rationale
Certain family members may collude with the perpetrator in order to keep the abuse/neglect secret; an objective interpretation is therefore required.

2.10   Take care not to assume prematurely that an elderly person is inadequately cared for, abused, or neglected, and do not suggest possible care plans prematurely.

Rationale
It is important not to superimpose the service professional's value judgements onto the elderly person: abuse or neglect is in the eye of the receiver. Offers of help may be premature and the required resource may not be at the disposal of the professional making the proposition.

Subsequent action

3.1   The police should be informed if it is suspected that a crime has been committed against person or property.

3.2   A referral should be made to the client's general practitioner or appropriate hospital medical staff so that a medical examination of the elderly person can be made immediately, with the informed consent of the elderly person. If injuries are found they should be mapped on a body chart.

Rationale
Evidence of injuries may be required in cases of charges being preferred for assault. In certain circumstances photographs may help the police in their inquiries (with the consent of the elderly

person). They may also help to understand the difficulties of diagnosing abuse/neglect from physical injuries.

3.3 Arrangements to protect an elderly person at risk must be made as soon as possible. A case conference involving all professionals concerned (and wherever possible the elderly person and caregiver) should be arranged within three working days and held within 10 working days. At this conference information will be fully shared, action planned, and a careful record made of the investigation and subsequent action.

3.4 If there is an urgent need to protect an abused or inadequately cared for elderly person, such an elderly person will have priority to obtain a bed in a residential unit provided he/she is willing to go. If medical care or an opinion as to the elderly person's competence to make such a decision is required, negotiations should be urgently undertaken through the elderly person's general practitioner or appropriate hospital medical staff to obtain this.

Registration

5.1 The case must be kept open and allocated to a social worker or other professional.

5.2 Efforts should be made to involve the elderly person in outside activities as appropriate to reduce risk and facilitate monitoring.

5.3 Respite care/phased care should be encouraged to reduce family conflict and facilitate monitoring.

5.4 Attempts should be made to put the elderly person in contact with a suitable advocate who can represent his/her interests.

5.5 If financial irregularity is suspected advice may be sought as appropriate from the elderly person's solicitor, bank manger/building society manager or Department of Social Security Office, who may undertake home visits to advise the elderly person. Application may be made to the Court of Protection in appropriate cases.

5.6 The case should be formally reviewed every six months (or earlier if applicable) while the elderly person remains in the situation in which the abuse/inadequate care occurred. The chairperson of the review should not hold line management responsibility for day-to-day case management.

Rationale
The chairperson, if a line manager, may be a 'gatekeeper' of services; therefore a conflict of interests may occur.

Records

Neighbourhoods will keep local records of cases of abuse/inadequate care of elderly persons registered. Such registers are intended to enable the department to check the numbers of such cases currently being reported and any trends that may be emerging. A record should be kept at the neighbourhood office of each such case with the name, address, age, date of birth, ethnic background, and the categories of abuse recorded, together with the date of the initial referral and initial case conference.

Staff support

Tower Hamlets Social Services recognizes that elderly persons at risk may sometimes remain in dangerous situations. Staff have access only to the Mental Health Act 1983 and Section 47 of the National Assistance Act 1948 (which will only apply in rare cases), and the Disabled Persons Act 1986. It may be that staff have no power to gain access to the elderly person, remove them from the situation, or investigate the conduct of affairs. Moreover the elderly person may refuse all help.

Rationale
Staff support is essential; the Americans have found that stress on service workers is high, especially in cases where interventions are continually refused [5].

This particular model will enable a rapid assessment followed by appropriate care planning (if required), co-ordination of services (if required) and consistent follow-up, within the stated aim of:

treating the care of an elderly person with the same urgency as that accorded child abuse.

There is clearly potential for health visitors, district nurses, community psychiatric nurses and practice nurses to develop expertise in elder abuse/inadequate care. The American experience would suggest that elder abuse assessment teams are one way of utilizing a multidisciplinary approach. The Beth Israel Assessment Team is just one example of a multidisciplinary organization designed to address the complex issues of elder abuse/inadequate care. Based within a large general hospital in Boston the team consists of nurses, physicians, and social workers. Their remit is to assess and evaluate referred cases of elder abuse/inadequate care. This team then reports to the appropriate authority with a suggested plan of care for the elderly person. Fulmer and O'Malley [6] suggest that this team approach has several assets:

- The suggested plan is individualized and takes into consideration the unique features of each case of abuse/inadequate care.
- The team is a group of experts each with individual expertise in the phenomenon of abuse/inadequate care.
- They are an asset to busy clinicians who suspect something is not right but do not have the expertise or time to assess for abuse/inadequate care.

One area of particular anxiety within the health arena is the accident and emergency department. American research suggests that considerable numbers of elderly people pass through emergency rooms with non-accidental injuries that are undetected [7]. Although the Beth Israel model may be useful in accident and emergency departments it could be utilized in any department, both health and social. When joint guidelines are developed it may be pertinent to identify an assessment team who could provide a consultative role within departments.

Many authorities will be in a position to use policy/procedures, albeit modified from the originals already in existence. What is vitally important is to review the workings of guidelines consistently. Because of the formative nature of the elder abuse/inadequate care debate we cannot assume the first answer will be the right answer. Dissemination of results from guidelines is also especially important. Individual authorities need to feed back consistently to and from other authorities in order to evaluate levels of:

- Suspected or proven abuse/inadequate care
- Methods of assessment
- Methods of intervention
- The degree of intervention success.

This information can then provide an information base on which policy strategy can be considered, both at a micropolitical level (individual authorities) and at a macropolitical level (Department of Health). This information will also frame the research agenda, which is also in its formative stages. One of the successes of the American experience of elder abuse/ inadequate care has been the production of statistics and analysis of State policy by the American Public Welfare Association [8]. This enabled individual States to compare and contrast both abuse/inadequate care levels and intervention policy. Beyond health and local authority guidelines, specific guidance is being produced by statutory and voluntary bodies. The multiagency document from Age Concern [9, 10] was a useful start in an attempt to formalize procedures. Initiatives continue to arrive with the latest from the Association of Directors of Social Services talking of *Adults at Risk* [11]. This change of emphasis suggests that adults as well as elders are potentially at risk, and the people they consider most at risk include those who:

- are elderly and very frail;
- suffer from mental illness, including dementia;
- have a learning disability;
- have a physical or sensory disability;
- suffer from severe physical illness.

Whilst this group may be potentially more at risk, it is wise to assume that elderly people without any disability may be victims of abuse/inadequate care. This will clearly be the case if we in Britain encounter the same research results as the Americans. These particular guidelines though only advisory will provide a much needed formalization to policy development. The guidelines suggest that:

> Directors are recommended to review their own procedures in the light of these guidelines. If no procedures exist, directors are recommended to arrange for their production as soon as possible. [11]

In order to provide a formalization of procedure/policy, development guidelines are required to mandate not only the local authorities but the health authorities to produce policies/procedures. This will require a Department of Health initiative. This acceptance of elder abuse/inadequate care as an official social problem worthy of assessment and intervention will only demand the resource required if it is legitimated by the Department of Health and agencies.

CASE MANAGEMENT

One extremely important aspect of the Government's White Paper on Community Care [12] relates to the concept of case management. Although this concept is not defined in the White Paper it is assumed that this type of service delivery offers advantages over present service delivery. One of the key objectives includes the proposal:

To make proper assessment of need and good quality case management the cornerstone of high quality care. [12]

Case management consists of:

1. Careful assessment of need
2. Comprehensive care planning
3. Co-ordination of services
4. Follow-up.

It has much in common with the key worker system which primary nursing embodies. Tyne [13], in espousing the principles of 'normalization', suggests that case management ensures services that are planned and co-ordinated around the needs of individuals in a flexible manner. Achieving this goal means that a case manager must take responsibility for the co-ordination of services while at the same time acting as the individual's guide and helper. Clearly this structure would suit intervention needs with abused and neglected elderly people. This framework of case-finding, planning, co-ordination, and monitoring assumes a degree of contact between case manager and the abused/neglected. This contact would be consistent with Lamb's [14] argument for 'case worker managers' to be therapists as well as brokers of service. Emphasis is thus placed on the role of helping the client through complex problems, and stresses the advantage of keeping the situation as simple as possible by enabling the same worker to form an important relationship with the client.

Perhaps the most difficult decision to be made with the case management model is the issue of who is the best placed professional to undertake this task. Sterthous [15] recommends the use of a small team consisting of a social worker and a nurse for the assessment and planning stages. Renshaw [16] argues that the most appropriate style of assessment will probably depend on the type of client. In cases where there are medical problems or liaison with health service agencies is required it may be necessary to employ nurses. It has become increasingly apparent over the last year that case management may not in fact fit any of the models so far suggested. However, what has been considered thus far are potential ideas that agencies may wish to explore, given the complexity of elder abuse and neglect.

It may be possible to solve this dilemma of who should case manage by using the elder abuse assessment team model. This assessment team could recommend which professional is best suited to provide case management. This model has previously been suggested by Zawadski and Eng [17] in order to differentiate the *brokerage model* from the preferred *consolidated model*.

- The brokerage model, where a professional assesses a frail elderly person, arranges services through other providers, and monitors and reassesses the individual regularly.
- The consolidated model, in which a multidisciplinary team assesses needs and then provides the required services. Zawadski and Eng point out that while the:

> brokerage model may be sufficient for a moderately impaired person with little or no informal support, a seriously impaired individual with a number of interrelated needs and limited informal support needs the consolidated model because of their multiple requirements and need for close monitoring.

This is precisely the point that Wolf and Pillemer [18] make when they suggest that:

All relevant agencies should be involved from the very

beginning in the design of a community elder abuse intervention.

The suggestion that case management can in fact be the service method which allows both health and social services to provide a multidisciplinary working team will be problematical. However, it is possible to work through some of these difficulties. Beardshaw and Towell [19] list some of the difficulties of merging case management and multidisciplinary work:

- Interprofessional rivalries can compromise effective working.

This may have been the case with other forms of community care; however, elder abuse/inadequate care does not have questions that any one professional can answer. In effect the American experience demanded almost a new worker in the Adult Protective Service specialist. It is suggested that no one professional will be prepared to tackle elder abuse alone. This may hopefully allow multipractitioner intervention if a holistic intervention is required. This liaison should start at the policy formulation stage if it is to work successfully.

- Interpretations of the key worker/case manager role may be coloured by particular professional backgrounds, with the result that clients receive a markedly different service depending on the key worker they have been assigned.

This is also a distinct possibility with interventions with elder abuse/inadequate care. Clearly the service intervention is in its formative stage in Britain, which gives an opportunity to design a unique intervention. One issue which will quickly demand interprofessional co-operation is the difficulty of differentiating age from disease from abuse (see Chapter 3).

This difficult task will demand at the least, medical, nursing, and social work intervention.

It will also require considerable co-operation between health and social authorities, which must again start at the policy formulation stage.

- Accessing resources within and across agencies may depend on negotiation with, and further assessment by, service managers.

This problem may in effect almost force the case manager to communicate cross-boundary. Clearly it is not the most effective method of co-operation; however, as has already been suggested elder abuse/inadequate care may not allow a single practitioner to solve the problem.

Wolf and Pillemer [18] in summing up the current state of the art in elder abuse/inadequate care suggest that:

> We have learned that coordinated, comprehensive services to abuse and neglected elders do work. . . . evaluations have demonstrated that direct services to victims and their families, coupled with a strong case-management role by a specialised elder abuse worker, have great potential to resolve maltreatment.

Clearly we must consider the American experience in some depth before we frame a response. Multiagency co-operation would seem to be crucial in this most demanding new social problem.

REFERENCES

1. Hildrew, M.A. (1991) *Guidelines on Elder Abuse: Which Social Services Departments Have Them.* BASW (Special Interest Group on Ageing).
2. Penhale, B. (In press) *Elder Abuse: New Findings and Policy Guidelines.* Paper Presented at Age Concern Ageing Update. 10 December 1992.
3. Kingston, P. (1990) Elder abuse. In *Elder Abuse: An Exploratory Study* (ed. McCreadie, C.). Age Concern Institute of Gerontology, King's College London.
4. Eastman, M. (1989) quoted in Tomlin, S. *Abuse of Elderly People: An Unnecessary and Preventable Problem.* British Geriatric Society.
5. Breckman, R.S. and Adelman, R.D. (1988) *Strategies for Helping Victims of Elder Mistreatment.* Sage, London.
6. Fulmer, T.T. and O'Malley, T.A. (1987) *Inadequate Care of the Elderly: A Health Care Perspective on Abuse and Neglect.* Springer Publishing Company, New York.
7. Jones, J. *et al.* (1988) Emergency department protocol for the diagnosis and evaluation of geriatric abuse. *Annals of Emergency Medicine*, 17 (10), 1006–15.
8. American Public Welfare Association/NASUA (1986) *A comprehensive analysis of state policy and practice related to elder abuse: A focus on role activities of state level agencies, inter-agency co-ordination efforts, public education/information campaigns.* Washington, DC.
9. Age Concern (1990) *Information for Carers.* Age Concern, UK.
10. Age Concern (1990) *Abuse of Elderly People: Guidelines for Action.* Age Concern, UK.

11. Association of Directors of Social Services (1990) *Adults at Risk: Guidance for Directors of Social Services.*

12. Department of Health (1989) *Caring for People: Community Care in the Next Decade and Beyond.* Cm 849, HMSO.

13. Tyne, A. (1981) *The Principles of Normalisation.* Campaign for Mentally Handicapped People.

14. Lamb, H. (1980) Therapist case managers: more than brokers of services. *Hospital and Community Psychiatry*, 31, 762–4.

15. Sterthous (1983) *Care Management: Variations on a Theme.* Mid-Atlantic Long-Term Care Gerontology Center, Philadelphia, PA, Temple University.

16. Renshaw, J. (1988) *Care in the Community.* Gower Publishing.

17 Zawadski, R.T. and Eng, C. (1988) Case management in capitated long-term care. *Health Care Financing Review Special Supplement.*

18. Wolf, R. and Pillemer, K.A. (1989) *Helping Elderly Victims.* Models Project Research, Columbia, New York.

19. Beardshaw, V. and Towell, D. (1990) *Assessment and Case Management: Implications for the Implementation of Caring for People.* Kings Fund Institute.

7

Prevention

Demographic realities mean that in the 1990s health care professionals will have to concentrate on the needs of the elderly, especially the frail 'oldest old'. Where will the prevention of elder abuse be in the pecking order of priorities? Much groundwork will need to be done in planning for the future care of the whole spectrum of older people and their carers in order to achieve the aim that elderly people should lead lives free from all forms of violence.

Some issues are already on the debating agenda and need to be addressed, including whether other vulnerable adults (e.g. mental handicap/learning disability) and institutional abuse (local authority Part III homes, hospital continuing care wards, and the private and voluntary sectors) should be included under the same sociological umbrella. Are there special and unique problems when researching a multiracial/multicultural society? One of the least explored areas of the topic is sexual abuse of the elderly, where even definitions are not available. Like many other unpalatable subjects, by its very nature it tends to be underreported.

The answers to some of these questions will be provided by carefully planned research projects. The data forthcoming should enable prevention strategies to be implemented and evaluated, modifying the approach as necessary.

SCREENING AS A MODEL FOR PREVENTION

The terms of the general practitioner (GP) contract require that elderly people over 75 years of age are offered an annual comprehensive health assessment. This obligation on GPs has produced renewed interest in the community care of elderly people and in particular the promotion of preventive health measures. The identification of disease, disability, and the implications of the social environment (which may greatly affect an individual's future wellbeing) provides the primary health care team with an opportunity to prevent potentially disastrous consequences. One particular area where this screening process could prove a valuable contribution to the holistic approach within community care is in the prevention of the abuse or inadequate care of dependent elderly people.

Although the prevalence of elder abuse in the UK remains unknown and difficult to determine, there is sufficient research evidence to suggest that the phenomenon is by no means insignificant. Estimates of prevalence vary but if the conservative figure of 4% is employed [1] this would translate as eight elderly people who are subjects of abuse or inadequate care within an elderly patient register of 200. Furthermore, although absolute age itself may not be a crucial factor in elder abuse, findings consistently point to a high proportion of victims aged over 75. In view of the relatively low level of awareness of elder abuse amongst health and social workers, preventive measures are at an early stage of development, if present at all. The over 75s screening process offers the possibility of alerting professionals, elderly people, their families, and carers to the high risk factors and situations associated with either present or future caring. The screening process could also serve as a useful indicator of the extent to which abuse and inadequate care is present amongst this age group in the community.

The screening process is usually performed by the GP or practice nurse. However, an initiative piloted by the Helen Hamlyn Research Unit involves training interviewers and combining the over-75s health check with the assessment process required in Care in the Community [2]. In screening for abuse and inadequate care the interviewer needs to be aware of the high risk factors summarized by Ogg and Bennett [3] and expanded in Chapter 2. The most important findings indicate a need to determine the quality of the family and caring relationships, and in particular the assessment of any dependencies on the part of the carer or other family members. If such high risk factors were found they would alert the primary health care team of the need to explore further with the elderly person their social network and the quality of the caring relationship.

Identification of high risk factors at an early stage and intervention to try to resolve them may lessen the possibility of abuse or inadequate care occurring.

Many situations of abuse and inadequate care reveal unmet needs and unknown demands on the part of the carer. The focus of the screening process may therefore necessarily shift later to an assessment of the carer's needs. The introduction of caring/support counselling by a member of the primary health care team may only be a partial resolution to an abusive relationship if there are other significant needs and demands on the part of the carer. For example, alcohol abuse by a carer requires a specific intervention. In some cases alcohol rehabilitation may be possible, or rehousing for either the carer or the elderly person may be an option. The alternatives available, however, are usually limited. Some practitioners are finding protocols such as high risk factor worksheets valuable tools to aid the assessment process [4].

In addition to being familiar with the high risk factors at the time of screening, the primary health care team need to be aware of the possibility of abuse or inadequate care occurring later in the caring role. Where there is evidence of progressive disease or increasing disability in the client, it is highly probable that family members will take a major role in planning for the future. Often the immediate family are contemplating how they can increase their caring role. Options such as siblings moving in to live with their elderly parents, or families asking their elderly relative to join their own home are frequently discussed.

Many families are unaware of the long and difficult task that a commitment to care entails, and decisions to enter into a caring relationship are often made in the absence of any counselling concerning the implications. Such decisions may have been made due to 'professional' advice with thoughtless remarks such as 'your mother must not be left alone', etc. As a consequence lives can be adversely changed, marriages ruined, and employment given up on the strength of these careless recommendations.

The screening process provides an opportunity to identify whether major life changes are envisaged and thought through by the elderly person and their family. Assessment instruments such as the 'Cost of Care Index' (Table 7.1) can help families

Table 7.1 The Cost of Care Index items*

---

1. I feel that my elderly relative is (will be) an overly demanding person to care for.
2. I feel that caring for my elderly relative puts (will put) a strain on family relationships.
3. I feel that caring for my elderly relative disrupts (will disrupt) my routine in my home.
4. I feel that caring for my elderly relative interferes (will interfere) with my friends or friends of my family coming to my home.
5. I feel that caring for my elderly relative has negatively affected (will negatively affect) my family's or my physical health.
6. I feel that caring for my elderly relative has negatively affected (will negatively affect) my appetite.
7. I feel that caring for my elderly relative has caused me (will cause me) to be physically fatigued.
8. I feel that caring for my elderly relative has caused me (will cause me) to become anxious.
9. I feel that meeting the psychological needs of my elderly relative for feeling wanted and important is not (will not be) worth the effort.
10. I feel that meeting the health needs of my elderly relative is not (will not be) worth the effort.
11. I feel that meeting the daily needs of my elderly relative is not (will not be) worth the effort.
12. I feel that meeting the social needs of my elderly relative for companionship is not (will not be) worth the effort.
13. I feel that my elderly relative is (will be) an overly demanding person to care for.
14. I feel that my elderly relative tries (will try) to manipulate me.
15. I feel that caring for my elderly relative has caused (will cause) my family and me much aggravation.
16. I feel that my elderly relative makes (will make) unnecessary requests of me for care.
17. I feel that caring for my elderly relative is causing me (will cause me) to dip into savings meant for other things.
18. I feel that my family and I must give up (will have to give up) necessities because of the expense of caring for my elderly relative.
19. I feel that my family and I cannot (will not be able to) afford those little extras because of the expense of caring for my elderly relative.
20. I feel that caring for my elderly relative is (will be) too expensive.

---

*Each item has a Likert-type response category. Items are randomly ordered in the actual CCI.

determine the emotional cost of caring and can be usefully employed to try to avoid future distress and recrimination [5]. Individuals are asked 20 questions which help them, in conjunction with an assessor, to decide whether the emotional costs of caring may be too high. Responses are scored on a scale of 1–4, a score of 1 indicating 'strongly disagree' through to 4 'strongly agree'. A maximum score of 80 points would indicate that potential or real stresses are present in the caring relationship. High scores which approach the maximum are also significant, although the interpretation of the index must be placed in the context of the total situation. Repeating the score over time may indicate a change in the caring circumstances.

Where the screening process identifies the socially isolated elderly person with no immediate family, the assessment needs to take account of potential risk situations which may lead to future inadequate care. Of crucial importance is the need to determine financial security. In addition to ensuring that a regular income is present, it is important to assess with the elderly person that management of their financial affairs is taking place appropriately. This is particularly relevant when dealing with confused elderly people. The mismanagement of finances over a long period of time can lead to chronic situations of unmet care needs.

Screening for elder abuse as part of the over-75s yearly health assessment could therefore produce positive preventive measures. As a general guide to its essential elements the primary health care team may find the following list useful:

- Be knowledgeable of the high risk factors associated with elder abuse and inadequate care.
- Be aware of the possibility of high risk factors that may present at a later date.
- Involve family and carers whenever possible in the screening process, but interview separately.
- Assessments take time, particularly with elderly people; be prepared to see someone on more than one occasion if the assessment indicates possible abuse or inadequate care. In complex cases use procedural guidelines where they are available and liaise with Social Services.
- Work closely with colleagues from other agencies.
- Introduce recording mechanisms that will alert the primary care team to changes over time. The real value of 'screening'

lies in its ability to detect significant changes throughout the ageing process.

ELDER SEXUAL ABUSE AS A MODEL FOR THE ISSUES AROUND PREVENTION

Professionals involved with the elderly are now identifying cases of elder sexual abuse by family members or other carers. Dependent elderly people who rely upon others for care appear to be especially vulnerable to sexual assault, and it is not the physical attributes but rather powerlessness and vulnerability which attract a sexual offender to a particular victim. Dependent elderly people, particularly those with speech, mobility, and other limitations, are very attractive as potential sexual abuse victims.

Studies of elder sexual abuse, intervention, and prevention are few. In one involving 52 cases of suspected sexual abuse 60% of the victims were dependent on care [6]. Almost all the victims were women and almost all the offenders men. Over 30% of the offenders were husbands caring for their dependent wives, forcing themselves sexually without consent. Almost 30% of the offenders were grown sons who sexually assaulted their elderly mothers. Other offenders included brothers, grandsons, lodgers, and non-related caregivers. The most common sexual assault was vaginal rape and in one-third of the cases repeated vaginal rape was suspected. Most of the cases were identified by specialist workers after they had been called in to assist elderly people who had suffered other forms of abuse by carers.

Ramsey-Klawsnik offers guidelines to professionals who may be involved in interviewing elderly people about possible sexual abuse.

- Become educated about elder sexual abuse; it makes interviewing easier.
- Be aware of the signs and symptoms – especially if a 'cluster' of symptoms occur.
- Interview the elderly person privately unless it is indicated that a 'trusted other' be present.
- Allow the person to have as much control over the interview as possible (choosing the place, seating arrangements, etc.).

- Treat the person with respect – one way includes calling the person by her surname, e.g. Mrs Jones.
- Don't take notes during the interview (wait until immediately after).
- Build rapport with non-threatening conversation and other methods before asking questions about possible sexual abuse.
- Proceed slowly and carefully, using speech and language appropriate to the person and situation.
- Ask questions singly and remind the person they can refuse one or all of the questions.
- Phrase questions in a non-leading, non-suggestive manner, which (if subsequently necessary) will not legally compromise the results of the interview. It is appropriate and necessary to ask direct questions.
- If a person discloses that he/she has been sexually abused, remain calm, thank the person, and ask to be told more about it. Assure the person that you will work to help his/her future safety from further sexual assault.
- Do not share your own emotions with your client.
- Ask clarifying questions (when and where, for how long, and what form of sex abuse activities). Identify anyone else involved.
- When appropriate use non-verbal means of communication such as anatomical dolls and anatomical drawings to elicit details of the abuse. This can be very helpful with those elderly people who suffer speech and language impairments, as well as with those who can communicate but are too embarrassed to use words to describe their assault(s).
- Tell victims that they are not alone, that this form of abuse happens to other older people. Explain that it is not their fault; they did not cause it.
- Refrain from expressing judgement towards the offender.
- Make a plan for the elder person's safety, encouraging decision making. Document all findings with a complete report.
- If the person denies sexual abuse but clinical evidence suggests the contrary, embarrassment or fear may be the cause. Give some relevant information, reassure and explain your concerns, indicating that you plan to return later to give him/her another opportunity to talk to you.

Ramsey-Klawsnik also lists myths regarding sexual abuse in an effort to ensure better preventive strategies.

Myths about victims

- Only females are sexually abused.
- Sexual assault occurs primarily in the lower socioeconomic groups.
- If the victim is not afraid or terrified of an abuser they have not been hurt by the assault.
- Disclosure then retraction indicates initial lying.
- After disclosure the story is easier to repeat, if not then the victim is lying.
- The victim of one episode of sexual abuse is not likely to allow it to happen again by the same person, or by anyone else.
- When incest occurs all family members are responsible (even the victim).
- All child victims of sexual abuse are at high risk of becoming abusers in the future.
- Victims 'get over' sexual abuse victimization by forgetting about it.
- Physical attributes and sexual desirability attract a sexual offender to a particular situation.

Myths about offenders

- Only males sexually abuse dependent others.
- An individual who adamantly and strenuously denies alleged sexual abuse and even willingly seeks services to 'prove' innocence must be innocent.
- Individuals who sexually abuse others have stopped engaging in consenting sexual relationships.
- One can know whether or not an individual could possibly sexually abuse by the individual's displayed behaviour and personality.
- Individuals who rape do so to achieve sexual gratification.

Myths about activities

- Sexual assault by a stranger is more traumatic than sexual abuse by a known and trusted other.

Table 7.2 Sexual abuse continuum (developed by H. Ramsey-Klawsnik)

Covert sexual abuse	Sexualized relationship
	   sexual interest in victim's body
	   sexualized jokes, comments, harassment
	   'romantic' relationship
	   discussion of sexual activity

Overt sexual abuse	Pre-touching phase
	   voyeurism
	   exhibitionism
	   inflicting pornography on victim

	Sexualized kissing and fondling
	   victim is passive recipient
	   victim activity is forced

	Oral–genital contact
	Digital penetration of vagina or anus
	Vaginal rape with penis
	Anal rape with penis
	Vaginal/anal rape with objects
	Exploitation
	Sadistic activity
	Ritualistic abuse

- Sexual abuse activities that are non-violent will do no lasting harm to the victim.
- Once an abuser is under supervision of the court or other authority, the chances of continued sexual abuse become very small.

Myths about professional services

- Most professional service providers (psychiatrists, psychologists, social workers, therapists, etc.) are trained to assess and treat sexual abuse.
- Families receiving mental health and or social work and other services cannot hide sexual abuse from the professional.

- Psychological testing of a sexual offender will reveal the individual's sexual dangerousness and potential to abuse.
- Psychological testing will reveal whether or not an individual has been sexually abused.
- Medical examination of the victim will usually reveal evidence of sexual abuse.

The Sexual Abuse Continuum (Table 7.2) developed by Ramsey-Klawsnik delineates the range and types of sexually abusive behaviour. It was developed from extensive experience interviewing child and adult victims of sexual violence. The continuum presents the activities typically described by victims listed in rank order from (generally) the least to the most severe in terms of degree of violence and trauma to the victim. Sexual abuse often begins with activities in the less severe range (if detected/acknowledged then allowing for possible prevention strategies) and escalates over time to more severe types of abuse. To constitute sexual abuse, the victim would have been forced, tricked, threatened, or otherwise coerced into the sexual contact against his or her will and without consent.

The authors are extremely grateful to Dr Holly Ramsey-Klawsnik for her permission to reproduce her work extensively.

Research: the key to preventive strategies

The use and relevance of US research data in the sociological field is often viewed with scepticism in the UK. The Americans are tarnished with broad brush strokes, violent, legalistic, and lacking in the concept of a welfare state and its implications. In the area of elder abuse, however, the US leads the way in the volume and depth of its research, and although some aspects may not travel well across the Atlantic we would be foolish indeed to disregard the main messages.

Pillemer and Finkelhor's seminal work in Boston [1] though criticized for some of its methodological approaches (initial telephone surveying) at least indicated a possible prevalence rate for elder abuse in the community. In the UK where the 1980s constructed the conservative new realism both Health and Social Services have been forced to heed the message that the need for new (or diversion of old) resources depends on a clear proof of that need. UK research in elder abuse is at an early stage, yet the groundwork is there. Ogg and Bennett [7], in the London Borough of Tower Hamlets, have modified Pillemer's methodology and are assessing the level of abuse in the community in this inner city area. With joint funded research monies and some charitable donations, a small team of researchers is interviewing a sample of residents aged over 65. The research population is drawn from hospital in-patients, day hospital attenders, day centre and luncheon club members, elderly people approached by their general practitioner, and residents of sheltered housing complexes. All potential responders are given information about the interview and written informed consent is obtained.

A structured interview schedule is then used, leading up to the Conflict Tactic Scale used by Pillemer to assess how families coped with certain issues including violence [4]. Tower Hamlets has a large Sylheti-speaking Bangladeshi population and a separate arm to the study involves researching evidence of elder abuse in this community.

The above study does not include elderly people suffering from chronic confusional states (for the obvious methodological reasons). However, this group of people is thought to be significantly at risk and their carers are particularly prone to stress. Homer and Gilleard opened up this debate concerning carers in an important study [8]. Bennett and Ogg are hoping to expand this knowledge base by interviewing the carers of people with chronic confusion and/or severe physical frailty, applying the same Conflict Tactic Scale as in the main study but this time geared to the carer. Both studies involve new ethical dilemmas for researchers, and indeed were only passed by the relevant Ethical Committee after much thought, debate, and modification. This topic is certainly at the 'cutting edge' of sociomedical research.

Community prevalence rates (albeit undoubtedly an underestimate) and prevalence rates in certain key groups (elderly mentally ill, severely physically frail, ethnic minority groups) will enable sensible prevention strategies to be made. Knowing the size of the problem, even in ball-park terms, at least helps in the rationalization of resources and focuses attention to the key areas of greatest need for further education and research. Intervention and prevention models will hopefully be as diverse as the situations generating them. These models will, however, need to be grouped together and evaluated in a research format to ensure the safety and quality of the caring response.

PREVENTION AND INTERVENTION: THE US APPROACH

One key feature in the US experience concerning possible prevention strategies is the elderly person's place of residence as it relates to issues of theory and prevention. Using this approach the elderly are subdivided into three broad groups (some with further subdivisions):

1. Elderly people living at home alone

This group falls outside of the theoretical models of stressed caretaker, psychopathology of the abuser, and transgenerational violence. They do not feature largely in the US research, and Fulmer and O'Malley wonder if this is due to a true lower incidence, or failure to meet the study definition [9]. These elderly people can receive inadequate care and it can be for a variety of reasons. The person may be unaware of a particular service or be unable to 'tap-in' because of physical or mental frailty. Neglect may be self-inflicted because of a distrust of others, or a mental illness, or it may be due to the failure of the 'system' to meet a person's needs. This failure may be professional (medical, social) or on the part of neighbours or family carers. The result is often insidious, however, eventually leading to increasing dependency and failing health.

Recognition and early intervention can prevent an otherwise inevitable decline towards institutionalization. Access to the person is crucial and can be difficult, requiring a lot of skilled work. Services need to be readily available and easy to obtain. This involves transport, home services, and possibly the use of an advocate to fight for the person's rights, and ensure provision, often in the face of at best apathetic or at worst hostile responses. Lessening social isolation is a key theme involving the building of new housing (with clustered facilities) and good-neighbour programmes, telephone help-lines, etc.

2. Elderly people living at home with others

(a) Caregivers;
(b) Non-caregivers.

Those elderly people living at home with carers (spouse, children, grandchildren, friends, paid carer) are thus dependent upon them for a service. Thus each of the theoretical models of abuse can apply. If carer stress is involved the carer's needs must be urgently assessed and both client and carer helped. This may involve counselling, day-care, respite care or even rehousing. Abuse/inadequate care resulting from psychopathology of the abuser will aim the intervention and prevention strategy at the carer. This may involve counselling, alcohol abuse clinic attendance, or removal to a drug/alcohol rehabilitation centre. In extreme circumstances the elderly person may need to be removed to a place of safety. Transgenerational violence as the cause of abuse may include situations where advice from the police is indicated.

The second group usually includes elderly people who are fairly physically and mentally fit, living with family members for one reason or another. The psychopathology of the abuser theory and the transgenerational violence theory can apply in these situations. The request for help may come from the elderly person or from outside the home, and each situation will have to be carefully and sensitively assessed. Workers have found that bringing in an outsider to try to help the home situation does reduce abuse independently of any contribution they may make to caring (exchange theory). Fulmer and O'Malley [9] also feel that an approach to reduce the dependency of the abuser on the elderly person (especially financial support) would be for the formal development of payment to family members or others to allow them to care. As they point out, many families give up work or lower their income in order to provide care.

3. Institutional settings

Local authority homes
Long-stay (continuing care) hospital
Private and voluntary sector.

There is no doubt (and we are frequently reminded of it by press and TV scandals) that abuse/inadequate care can and does occur in institutional settings. Local authority homes and continuing care wards in hospitals should be regularly visited and audited by the relevant statutory agency. Standards do indeed vary but should not fall below recognized norms. Previous scandals have highlighted the importance of good leadership, sufficient well-trained and motivated staff, suitable accommodation, and ongoing audit and education. Despite a string of horror stories in both health and social service institutions, the level of care remains basic in most establishments. Inadequate pay results in too few staff barely motivated to continue in the job, let alone receive 'training'. Staff turnover is high, resident dependency levels are increasing, and quality of care becomes an issue to aim at rather than achieve.

The private and voluntary sector does have mandatory inspections but the general consensus is that these are too few and far between. The private sector can provide the goals to which other forms of care need to aspire but it can also produce the profit-seeking degradation of the old.

The sorry mess that the UK long-stay sector has found itself in is a direct result of the Conservative Government led backing of private institutions. Reform of the care of the chronically sick, disabled and frail was certainly needed. The answer should have been to provide a spectrum of care, modified locally, to provide elderly people with what they need and want. This spectrum would range from those requiring continuing care in hospital, to NHS nursing homes, hospital at home schemes, partnership homes (NHS and local authority providing dual facilities), local authority rest homes, and a private sector free to expand where it can but not because the public sector is penalized. The Government has spent billions of pounds just to promote the private sector and forced both local authority and health services to buy into this operation. This does not produce choice for the consumer; it results in elderly people being shunted around the country finding a funded place. So much expertise within the health and social services has been squandered by refusing to give them a slice of the cake with the remit to provide good-quality care, the ideology borders on the criminal.

Standards can be improved in all establishments by the introduction of a resident's bill of rights or charter. Residents or their advocates could then ensure that quality and standards of care were adhered to. Abuse theories can apply in institutions. Impairment theories and stressed carer theories can result in a careworker being overwhelmed in the job. The psychopathology of the abuser and transgenerational violence theory may also apply (a care provider may be abusing alcohol or drugs or have a mental illness, making it inappropriate that he/she is in a caring role). Staff disciplinary measures should be in place, however, to help in such circumstances. The safety of the residents has to be addressed as well as an intervention strategy for the carer. National standard setting in all institutions would reduce the potential for abuse to occur. Sanctions must include the criminal law for both carer and the institution (see Chapter 8).

EDUCATION: ITS ROLE IN PREVENTION

There is a certain intrinsic wisdom in seeing the multidisciplinary approach as the only way forward in the prevention of elder abuse. There are already examples of good practice that indicate a constructive approach, e.g. the British Geriatrics Society (BGS) multidisciplinary conference in 1988 [10]. This meeting certainly enthused some individuals, who went back to their respective districts and raised the issue there. National multidisciplinary guidelines began appearing, including the British Association of Social Work (BASW) and The Royal College of Nursing (RCN) [11, 12]. In some districts the committed individuals from the BGS conference ensured that local guidelines were established [13], yet the total number of local authorities involved with elder abuse policy remains disappointly small [P. Kingston: *Elder abuse*. Unpublished MSc Dissertation, 1990] with even less interest by health authorities. In 1991 the Assistant Directors of Social Services (ADSS) produced a report [14] and early in 1992 the Social Service Inspectorate (SSI) [15] released the first stage of a two-stage publication concerning elder abuse with multidisciplinary workshops in various cities.

Conferences, workshops, etc. are now increasingly common, and are a vital first step in raising not only professional but also lay public awareness. This increased professional interest is mirrored in the growing number of articles, book chapters, and media reports. Eastman may be forgiven for a feeling of *déjà vu*; only time will tell if this renaissance is permanent. To avoid sublimation again I feel that two related phenomena must occur: a critical mass effect and a big bang!

There has never been a greater professional interest in the issue, yet small research projects are often duplicated unnecessarily while other important areas remain unexplored. This is because there are still comparatively few 'experts' in the field and general professional awareness is low outside the immediate areas within which these 'experts' work. Conferences and seminars only go a small way to solve this problem, as interested individuals may attend yet policy makers and training officers often do not. Legislation, governmental guidelines, enforced/compulsory policy, and comprehensive multidisciplinary staff training are still a long way away.

In the meantime a critical mass of interested professionals has to be generated in order to push the issue into the next phase of its development. One way of achieving this is via the establishment of a National Organization similar to that in the US: The National Committee for the Prevention of Elder Abuse [16]. To this effect a steering group was convened in February 1992 by Dr G. Bennett at The Royal London Hospital Trust. Acknowledged experts in the field indulged in a SWOT (strengths, weaknesses, opportunities, threats) analysis of such an organization and prioritized the evolving issues into a phased action plan. The need for such an organization was evident, with a clear responsibility to raise awareness in all sectors of society but initially to concentrate on its proposed professional membership; social work, medicine, nursing, law, research/academia, voluntary sector. The proposed organization was seen as having a crucial role in not only making professionals aware of the issues but also disseminating that important information via newsletters, conferences, articles, etc. Once established, the membership helps set many of the agenda issues and establishes links with other groups, especially the carers' organizations and bodies with strong carer profiles, e.g. the Alzheimer's Disease Society and the Parkinson's Disease Society.

A successful and dynamic organization can also raise public awareness concerning elder abuse and help make the climate appropriate for the next phase – the big bang. This involves the organization being recognized as the authority in the field and as such being approached by the media for responses and comments at key times. It involves the organization using the media to help raise awareness, but also being sensitive to the difficult nature of this activity. Successful prevention may involve the development of a telephone 'helpline' which has been adjudged such a success in child abuse. Local branches of the organization may be set up, becoming local pressure groups.

Many people believe that effective change will only occur via the political legislative route. This obviously involves immense multidisciplinary resources, especially the input of wise legal counsel. One acknowledged route for such pressure is through the Parliamentary lobbying system: sophisticated yet often very successful.

Once the quantum leap into a truly national debate has occurred, truly anything can happen. The end result can be effective change with a knock-on effect into other countries, especially Europe where similar demographic changes are occurring. Only hindsight will tell us if the 1990s resulted in elder abuse being considered on a par with the other examples of societal violence. The steering committee called together to discuss a national organization (Action on Elder Abuse) ended their deliberations by writing a mission/vision statement as their hope for the future. It reads:

> To prevent elder abuse by promoting changes in policy and practice through raising awareness, education, research and the dissemination of information.

REFERENCES

1. Pillemer, K.A. and Finkelhor, D. (1988) The prevalence of elder abuse. *The Gerontologist*, 28 (1), 51–7.
2. Department of Health (1989) *Caring for People: Community Care in the Next Decade and Beyond*, Cm 849, HMSO.
3. Ogg, J. and Bennett, G.C.J. (1991) Community care: identifying risk factors for elder abuse. *Geriatric Medicine*, 21 (11), 19.
4. Kosberg, J. (1988) Preventing elder abuse: identification of high risk factors prior to placement decisions. *The Gerontologist*, **28**, 43–50.
5. Kosberg, J. and Cairl, R. (1986) The cost of care index: a case management tool for screening informal care providers. *The Gerontologist*, 26 (3), 273–8.
6. Ramsey-Klawsnik, H. (1991) Elder sexual abuse: preliminary findings. *Journal of Elder Abuse and Neglect*, 3 (3), 73–90.
7. Ogg, J. and Bennett, G.C.J. (1991) Answering some of the questions posed by elder abuse. *Geriatric Medicine*, 21 (10), 15–16.
8. Homer, A. and Gilleard, C. (1990) Abuse of elderly people by their carers. *British Medical Journal*, 301, 1359–62.
9. Fulmer, T.T. and O'Malley, T.A. (1987) *Inadequate Care of the Elderly. A Health Care Perspective on Abuse and Neglect.* Springer Publishing Co., New York.

10. Tomlinson, S. (1988) *Abuse of elderly people: an unnecessary and preventable problem*. Public Information Report. British Geriatrics Society. September.
11. *Adults at Risk*, Parliamentary Briefing, BASW.
12. *Guidelines for Nurses: Abuse and older people*, Working Group Report, RCN.
13. Penhale, B. (1993) The abuse of elderly people: considerations for practice. *British Journal of Social Work*, **23** (2), 95–112.
14. *Adults at Risk: Guidance for Directors of Social Services*. (1991) Association of Directors of Social Services.
15. *Confronting Elder Abuse*. Dept. of Health (Social Services Inspectorate), HMSO, 1992.
16. *National Committee for the Prevention of Elder Abuse*. The Medical Center of Central Massachusetts, Institute on Aging, 119 Belmont St. Worcester, MA 01605, USA.

8

Institutional abuse and neglect

Although the main emphasis in this book has been centred on elder abuse and neglect within the domestic setting, the phenomenon of institutional abuse and neglect needs consideration. Britain along with other countries, America, Germany, and Israel, has a history of abuse in institutions that care for elderly people, including those with mental health impairments [1–8]. The phenomenon undoubtedly exists in other countries where there are institutions for elderly people. The abuse and neglect appears in all types of settings including:

Elderly care wards in National Health Service hospitals
Private nursing homes
Private residential homes
Local Authority Part III accommodation
Voluntary sector homes

Many of the scandals can be traced to practices consistent with the Poor Laws of the nineteenth century. However, it was not until the text 'Sans Everything: A Case to Answer' [2] was published in 1967 that the issue of institutional malpractice was taken seriously. This text was a commentary on the inadequacies of elderly care in hospitals around Britain. Although it prompted enquiries into these failings, a major initiative to improve the standards in elderly care was woefully lacking. Alongside the short-term remedies that seem to follow each scandal, there is a deficiency in research that could be used to explain and remedy the socialization processes that lead to such scandals. Few authors since Goffman [9] have looked inside the 'total institution'; the few that have will be reviewed. Phillipson [10] suggests that one of the reasons for the paucity of research is the 'failure to give proper weight to abuse in institutional settings' *vis-à-vis* abuse in domestic settings. Research on domestic abuse is rare enough in Britain, and it is no surprise that American research seems to give more answers about the causation of, and remedies for, institutional abuse.

The spectrum of abusive and neglectful behaviours encountered in elderly care institutions is remarkably varied. Studies have considered the basic standards of privacy [11], the physical care and quality of life [12], the erosion of individuality in the care of elderly people in hospital [13], resistance to change in geriatric care [14], the physical working conditions in hospitals [15], nursing staff burn-out [16], organizational factors leading to low standards of care [17], fraud in nursing homes [4], and the taking of life in old people's homes [7]. A critical American overview of the literature regarding abuse of patients in nursing homes is provided by Pillemer [5].

Pillemer's model will be used to frame an analysis of institutional abuse presented in the literature to date, utilizing an international perspective. Although this particular framework considers 'nursing homes', the findings are considered to be generic enough to be used as a template for most 'elderly care institutions', irrespective of sector (public, private, voluntary, and whether nursing or residential). The first difficulty Pillemer encounters is a definitional one; not surprising as this is also one of the major difficulties in the domestic elder abuse and neglect debate. However, there are expected standards of care within institutions (although these may vary internationally/ nationally and even locally), usually mandated by law. The system of registration in Britain is controlled by the regulations embodied in 'The Nursing Homes and Mental Nursing Homes Regulations' [18], and the quality of care within residential establishments is outlined in 'Home Life' [19]. Guidance documents are also available [20, 21]. He also suggests that a definition of maltreatment can be developed by considering deviations from expected standards. Pillemer considers four interrelated variables that may account for maltreatment:

Exogenous factors
Nursing home environment
Staff characteristics
Patient characteristics

EXOGENOUS FACTORS

Exogenous factors are external to the care facility. Pillemer suggests two particular factors: the supply and demand of nursing home beds and the unemployment rate. Homes in areas where there is an excess of beds will often accept patients without any formal assessment. Patients can therefore be misplaced and very early in the caring process practitioners are called in to 'sort the situation out'. In the worst circumstances the patient or the patient's relatives are told to find another placement. From the consumer's point of view areas with excess beds allow the client/relative to 'shop around' to find the highest quality. Areas with a shortage of beds (especially specialist beds for the elderly mentally ill) can almost always fill their beds, even with a reputation for poor-quality care. Carers of elderly people with dementia often wait for a vacancy to arise in a registered Mental Nursing Home because of the shortage of beds. The volume of private beds within a District Health Authority may influence the decision to close a particular home. Very few District Health Authorities could find 50 beds for elderly people overnight if a private home required closure. This may constrain members of the registration body, giving homes extra time to bring their quality up to standard when closure is the correct option.

The unemployment rate and rates of pay may affect staffing levels. In periods of unemployment homes may be able to choose staff with higher qualifications than in periods of relatively high employment. However, if rates of pay are low, staff may leave at short notice and unfilled vacancies have a 'knock-on' motivational affect which will affect other workers [22]. At a macro-policy level in Britain today the changes towards a 'market forces' care sector for elderly people has been viewed as:

> Mass abuse of vulnerable elderly people by Social Service Departments and the comparative acquiescence of the social work profession in it can only be understood in terms of the concept of Institutionalised Ageism.

Jack [23] was referring to the consistent transfer of elderly people from Local Authority homes to the private sector at a time when there are increasing reports of abuse arising out of the private sector [11, 22, 28]. Chambers portrays a disturbing

Table 8.1 Macrosociological factors affecting conditions in nursing homes

---

- Advances in medical technology which prolong life but do not cure disease [24].
- The increased severity of illness found in nursing homes. (This is certainly the case in Local Authority homes [12].)
- A Congress bent on deficit reduction and therefore not open to increased funding of nursing homes. (In Britain, see 'Who Cares Who Pays' [25].)
- A dearth of physicians who are sensitive to the special needs of the elderly.
- A market economy not given to national health insurance but supportive of a system of investor-owned nursing home corporations which tend to hire relatively unskilled labour. (See [22] in Britain.)

---

picture of how abuse/neglect can occur in the private sector when minimum standards are not enforced; her recommendations include:

> Minimum standards could be enforced by the threat of closure. . . . Comprehensive inspections should be made frequently and without prior notice. . . . Attending General Practitioners and other visiting professionals might be asked to report on the running of the home. [22]

Clearly policy formulation can be considered to have a profound effect on the quality of elderly care. Wiener and Kayser-Jones point to several American 'macro-sociological' conditions that influence the organizational conditions in nursing homes [17]. It is useful to consider how many of these conditions in a pluralistic health system like America can be found to be influencing the quality of elderly care in Britain (Table 8.1).

Wiener and Kayser-Jones [17] make the point that:

> Most of these constraints require massive national attention. . . . despite the severe impact of external conditions, for the most part they are not in the consciousness of the crucial actors within the nursing home scene.

This point is central to the debate surrounding the quality of care in elderly residential establishments. Many improvements can be made from within these institutions; however, on a macro-scale, policy changes to address the phenomenon of 'institutional ageism' explored by Jack [23] are required. Elder abuse and neglect can further be explored using the political economy perspective on ageing [26–28]. This perspective suggests that elderly people are treated and processed as commodities; their dependency is in fact socially constructed by enforced passivity. They are not considered consumers of services but rather endurers of the services that stigmatize and segregate them:

> Retirement, poverty, institutionalisation and restriction of domestic community roles are the experiences which help explain the structured dependency of the elderly. [26]

NURSING HOME ENVIRONMENT

Pillemer considers the term 'environment' to include the physical design of the building, and its organizational structure, range and intensity of services, alongside the facility's economic resources.

Physical design

In *Private lives in Public Places* [29] an evaluation of 100 public-sector homes was reported. One of the questions raised was: Has the residential home been designed with the needs of the residents or staff in mind? The answer given at the end of the discussion claims:

> Our description . . . begins to confirm the reality of the home as an institution where the needs of the organisation have to be met . . . the physical environment has not been designed to take into account residents' lifestyles.

Within the elderly care provision of the National Health Service a wide variation in environmental quality is reported [15]:

> During our visits we saw nurses trying to rehabilitate patients in wards that were unsuitable. We also saw standards of ward decoration and upkeep that were a disgrace to a civilised nation. In contrast we saw wards which had been upgraded imaginatively, colour co-ordinated and which were immaculately clean.

Fleishman and Ronen [8] report long-term care institutions having:

> poor physical conditions, these include overcrowded rooms, a shortage of toilets, no elevators, and the absence of heating and hot water.

Organization structure

Much has been written about the organizational structure that leads to poor quality of care and sometimes abuse and neglect. Frequently the term 'custodial orientation' appears as a general description of life within the institution. The work by Goffman [9], though over 30 years old, presents a vivid picture of what can still be found in the 'total institution':

> First, all aspects of life are conducted in the same place and under the same single authority. Second . . . daily activity is carried out in the immediate company of a large batch of others. Third, all phases of activity are tightly scheduled. Finally the various enforced activities are brought together . . . purportedly designed to fulfil the official aims of the Institution.

Examples taken from British research include a caseworker entering a resident's room with a matron, who then opened the resident's window; when the resident complained of the cold the matron stated that the window should remain open to freshen the room [11]. Residents being woken and dressed at 0530 [12]; the rationale is usually that the day staff do not have sufficient time to get all the residents dressed in time for breakfast. Conveyor-belt systems [12] are often used starting at one end of a corridor and working along, dressing a resident and then taking him/her to the day room, sometimes for a two-hour wait until breakfast [12]. 'Toileting' is another process that can be turned into a conveyor-belt routine. Even the expression 'toileting' is infantalizing. Descriptions of the toileting process include:

> Each stage of the process was conducted by a different member of staff. . . . The toilet had no doors. Soiled clothes were stripped off the individual . . . and tossed into a communal bin. The entire process was regimented, dehumanising and

completely without privacy, although this is not to say that staff were brusque, cold or uncaring.

Practices with a history from the workhouse often remain in place, including the 'bath book'. Residents are entered in the book at the beginning of the week and must have at least one bath. Staff use the gaps between other tasks to bathe the residents until all the names are ticked of the list. Residents are not asked when they would wish to bathe, but slotted in between other tasks. Kayser-Jones writes of the:

> . . . dehumanizing experiences centred around bathing and elimination. . . . Patients having their genitals exposed, bathing men and women simultaneously in the same shower room.

This general malaise in certain institutions actually results in low expectations from both staff and residents. Counsel and Care [11] comment that they were: 'struck by their [residents'] generally low expectations and by the absence of protest'. Wiener and Kayser-Jones [17] talk of the 'downward spiral' which affects patients, staff and relatives as they become aware of 'their powerlessness to effect change'.

STAFF CHARACTERISTICS

British research on staff characteristics found in poor-quality residential settings is hard to find. However, anecdotal reports exist. Staff in charge of the now infamous Nye Bevan Lodge [30] were considered to be:

> Very committed, caring and hardworking, but had no managerial training.

How can it be that these same individuals worked in a residential home where patients were 'made to eat their own faeces, left unattended, physically manhandled, forced to pay money to care staff and even helped to die'? [30]. Harman and Harman report many more examples of physical abuse and verbal aggression [31].

The American work by Pillemer and Bachman-Prehn [32] suggests certain variables that may be found among staff who are perpetrators of abuse and neglect.

1. *Education.* Early research suggests that staff with low levels of education hold more negative attitudes towards the elderly [33]. This correlates to Jack's [23] suggestion that few qualified social workers opt to work in the elderly care field, quoting Borsay [34]:

   First child care, second mental health, thirdly the elderly.

   Research by Slevin [35] suggests that entry into nursing did not lead to a more positive attitude; rather it had a converse effect. It may be that traditional nurse training reinforced negative attitudes held before entering the profession. In a recent unpublished study by Woods evidence appears to suggest that this phenomenon could be abated and that in part this may be attributable to a shift in the educational philosophy of nurse education. With the advent of Project 2000, nurse educators have moved away from the reactive medical model as a basis for nursing care toward a pro-active, health and wellbeing approach to nurse education.
2. *Age.* Older staff members were found to have less negative attitudes to the elderly [36].
3. *Position.* Ethnographic research by Kayser-Jones [6] suggests that nursing aides are often the staff who resort to abuse. Similar findings were reported when the Report of the Inquiry into Nye Bevan Lodge [37] was published. The report suggests that a core group of care assistants supported by trade unions proved difficult to change in terms of their working practices.
4. *Burn-out.* The term burnout has been around for a number of years, yet little research is available to substantiate the leading factors. Heine [16] considers that the end product of burn-out involves

   . . . Physical, emotional and spiritual exhaustion and ultimately involves the loss of concern with whom one is working.

PATIENT CHARACTERISTICS

Health of patients

Many of the scandals of abuse that occur involve mentally impaired elderly people. In other areas (learning disabilities) this is also the case. Vousden [30] suggests that the residents of Part III homes have different needs from those originally envisaged. Greater levels of impairment both physical and mental are common in these local authority homes. It may be that the staff either are not skilled to deal with these levels of impairment or do not wish to work with highly dependent elders [38]. The ability to complain is an important factor. When elderly people have the ability to complain and believe their complaints will be listened to, there is less chance of abuse.

Social isolation

This is clearly a risk factor for domestic abuse. It may be that elderly people who have regular visitors in residential care may be at less risk of abuse. Certainly, visitors who take their relative's clothes home for cleaning, bring in extra food, and visit frequently are probably more aware of the individual behaviours of their relative and more in tune with the ambience of the home. This will enable the relatives to notice subtle changes in their relative's behaviour, which they may ask the staff about.

Having considered a broad spectrum of variables that may promote and reinforce abuse, the question of how often this abuse occurs needs consideration. No prevalence figures are available on the levels of abuse and neglect in Britain; however, cases that arrive at the Registered Homes Tribunal shed some light on how many individual homes are guilty of abusive/ neglectful practices [31]. There still remains, however, some truth in Kahana's statement from 20 years ago:

> Those few accounts which look at the quality of life in institutions for the aged at close range tend to conjure up images of Dante's Inferno. . . . Nevertheless there are no hard data on the prevalence of inhumane treatment in various institutional settings. Consequently there is the possibility that we are interpreting the isolated or occasional event as the norm. [39]

A self-reported prevalence study from America [40] used a telephone survey to assess levels of observed physical and psychological abuse alongside abuse (physical and psychological) actually committed by the nursing staff. A sample of 577 nurses responded to the telephone interviews (61% nursing aides, 20% licensed practical nurses, and 19% registered nurses). The interview schedule was based on the Conflict Tactics Scale [41].

Staff reports of abuse by others

It can be seen from Tables 8.2–8.5 that 36% of the nursing staff had observed physical abuse in the preceding year. Psychological abuse was observed by 81% of the nurses in the previous year. These are quite startling figures, especially because there is a tendency to underreport abusive acts in order to report socially desirable responses. When the figures on staff reporting their own actions are also considered, the concern becomes all the greater.

Table 8.2 Physical abuse observed by staff in past year ($N = 577$)

Type of abuse	Never	Once	2–10 times	More than 10 times
Excessive use of restraints	79%	6%	9%	6%
Pushed, grabbed, shoved, or pinched	83%	7%	9%	1%
Slapped or hit	88%	6%	6%	—
Threw something	97%	2%	1%	—
Kicked or hit with fist	98%	1%	1%	—
Hit or tried to hit with object	98%	1%	1%	—

Table 8.3 Psychological abuse observed by staff in past year ($N = 577$)

Type of abuse	Never	Once	2–10 times	More than 10 times
Yelled at patient in anger	30%	11%	44%	15%
Insulted or swore at	50%	9%	30%	11%
Isolated patient inappropriately	77%	7%	12%	4%
Threatened to hit or throw at	85%	5%	9%	1%
Denied food or privileges	87%	2%	8%	3%

Table 8.4 Physical abuse committed by staff in past year (N = 577)

Type of abuse	Never	Once	2–10 times	More than 10 times
Excessive use of restraints	94%	3%	2%	1%
Pushed, grabbed, shoved, or pinched	97%	2%	1%	—
Slapped or hit	97%	2%	1%	—
Hit or tried to hit with object	98%	1%	1%	—
Threw something	99%	—	1%	—
Kicked or hit with fist	100%	—	—	—

Table 8.5 Psychological abuse committed by staff in past year (N = 577)

Type of abuse	Never	Once	2–10 times	More than 10 times
Yelled at patient in anger	67%	15%	17%	1%
Insulted or swore at	90%	4%	5%	1%
Denied food or privileges	96%	1%	2%	1%
Isolated patient inappropriately	96%	2%	2%	—
Threatened to hit or throw at	98%	1%	1%	—

Tables 8.2–8.5 are reproduced by permission from *The Gerontologist*, Reference [40].

Staff reports of own abusive actions

A total of 10% of the nurses admitted committing one or more physically abusive acts, with 40% admitting to psychological abuse.

Pillemer, in analysing these findings, claims that the view that abusive incidents are isolated may be inaccurate, and that in fact abuse may be widespread and a relatively regular part of institutional life.

CONCLUSION

The relative absence of research suggesting institutional abuse appears to portray a false picture of the quality of care in elderly residential care. A rather more disturbing picture is depicted by the findings of the 'First Ninety-six Cases of the Registered Homes Tribunal' [31]. This picture is indeed validated by the findings of the *Report of the Inquiry into Nye Bevan Lodge* [37]. The research agenda is wide open at this point in time. Urgent replication of studies similar to Pillemer's [40] are required, albeit with modified methodology (see Chapter 9).

Various authors have suggested ways to address quality in the residential sector [42, 43]. However, it has been suggested in this chapter that certain variables that have a direct correlation with quality are outside the parameters of the residential building. Therefore changes at two levels are required. Firstly research that has concentrated within the framework of the home environment needs utilizing by care staff in order to address issues of quality. The recent work of Gibbs and Sinclair [44] clearly highlighted four correlates of quality:

1. Head of home – quality depends on leadership.
2. Staffing – quality would depend on numbers, qualifications and morale.
3. Resident dependency – quality would depend on the proportions of severely dependent residents being catered for by adequate staff numbers.
4. Buildings – quality depends on the suitability of the buildings.

At a macro-political level the concept of 'institutionalized ageism' [23] needs strong attention and action. Phillipson and Walker offer a radical perspective that all carers should heed:

> In social policy terms, the task over the next ten years is to break the link between growing old and becoming dependent. This will involve action on both political and economic fronts; but it will also involve . . . a challenge to our work as carers – in both formal and informal settings. Crucially it will demand that older people become centrally involved in the planning and administration . . . of their welfare state. [45]

REFERENCES

1. Martin, J.P. (1984) *Hospitals in Trouble*. Oxford, Basil Blackwell.
2. Robb, B. (1967) *Sans Everything: A Case to Answer*. Thomas Nelson, Edinburgh.

3. Townsend, P. (1962) *The Last Refuge.* Routledge, London.
4. Halamandaris, V.J. (1983) Fraud and abuse in nursing homes. In *Abuse and Maltreatment of the Elderly: Causes and Interventions* (ed. Jordan Kosberg). John Wright, Bristol.
5. Pillemer, K. (1988) Maltreatment of patients in nursing homes: overview and research agenda. *Journal of Health and Social Behavior,* 29 (3), 227–38.
6. Kayser-Jones, J. (1981) *Old, Alone and Neglected: Care of the Aged in Scotland and the United States.* University of Los Angeles Press, Berkeley, CA.
7. Dissenbacher, H. (1989) Neglect, abuse and the taking of life in old people's homes. *Ageing and Society,* 9 (1), 61–72.
8. Fleishman, R. and Ronen, R. (1989) Quality of care and maltreatment in israel's institutions for the elderly. In *Stress, Conflict and Abuse of the Elderly* (ed. Wolf, R.S. and Bergman, S.). JDC–Brookdale Monograph Series, Jerusalem.
9. Goffman, E. (1961) *Asylums.* Doubleday, New York.
10. Phillipson, C. (In press) Abuse of older people: sociological perspectives. In *The Mistreatment of Elderly People* (ed. Glendenning, F. and DeCalmer, P.). Sage Publications, London.
11. Counsel and Care (1991) *Not Such Private Places.* Counsel and Care, London.
12. Hughes, B. and Wilkin, D. (1989) Physical care and quality of life in residential homes. *Ageing and Society,* 7 (4), 399–425.
13. Kenny, T. (1990) Erosion of individuality in care of elderly people in hospital: an alternative approach. *Journal of Advanced Nursing,* 15, 571–6.
14. Smith, G. (1986) Resistance to change in geriatric care. *International Journal of Nursing Studies,* 23 (1), 61–70.
15. Millard, P. and Roberts, A. (1991) Old and forgotten. *Nursing Times,* 87 (22), 24–8.
16. Heine, C. (1986) Burnout among nursing home personnel. *Journal of Gerontological Nursing,* 12, 14–18.
17. Wiener, C.L. and Kayser-Jones, J. (1990) The uneasy fate of nursing home residents: an organisational-interaction perspective. *Sociology of Health and Illness,* 12 (1), 84–104.
18. *The Nursing Homes and Mental Nursing Homes Regulations* (1984). HMSO, London.
19. *Home Life: A Code of Practice for Residential Care* (1984) Centre for Policy on Ageing.
20. *Guidance on Standards for Residential Homes for Elderly People* (1990) HMSO, London.
21. *National Association of Health Authorities, Registration and Inspection of Nursing Homes* (1985) National Association of Health Authorities.
22. Chambers, R. (1991) The power and the 'gory' of private care homes. *Care of the Elderly,* 3 (8), 356.
23. Jack, R. (1992) Institutionalised elder abuse, social work and social service departments. *Baseline,* No 50, 24–7.
24. Callahan, D. (1987) *Setting Limits: Medical Goals in an Aging Society.* Simon and Schuster, New York.

25. Peaker, C. (1988) *Who Cares Who Pays*. National Council of Voluntary Organisations.
26. Townsend, P. (1986) Ageism and social policy. In *Ageing and Social Policy: A Critical Assessment* (ed. Phillipson, C. and Walker, A.). Gower, Aldershot.
27. Phillipson, C. (1982) *Capitalism and the Construction of Old Age*. Macmillan, London.
28. Walker, A. (1981) Towards a political economy of old age. *Ageing and Society*, 1 (1), 73–94.
29. Willcocks, D., Peace, S. and Kellaher, L. (1987) *Private Lives in Public Places*. Tavistock Publications, London.
30. Vousden, M. (1987) Nye Bevan would turn in his grave. *Nursing Times*, 83 (32), 18–19.
31. Harman, H. and Harman, S. (1989) *No Place Like Home*. NALGO, London.
32. Pillemer, K. and Bachman-Prehn, R. (1991) Helping and hurting: predictors of maltreatment of patients in nursing homes. *Research on Aging*, 13 (1), 74–95.
33. White, C.M. (1977) The nurse–patient encounter: Attitudes and behaviours in action. *Journal of Gerontological Nursing*, 3, 16–20.
34. Borsay, A. (1989) First child care, second mental health, third the elderly. *Research Policy and Practice*, 7 (2).
35. Slevin, O.D. (1991) Ageist attitudes among young adults: implications for a caring profession. *Journal of Advanced Nursing*, 16, 1197–205.
36. Penner, L.A., Lederria, K. and Mead, G. (1984) Staff attitudes: image or reality? *Journal of Gerontological Nursing*, 10, 110–17.
37. *Report of the Inquiry into Nye Bevan Lodge* (1987) Southwark Social Services, London.
38. Biggs, S. (1989) Professional helpers and resistances to work with older people. *Ageing and Society*, 9 (1), 43–60.
39. Kahana, E. (1973) The humane treatment of old people in institutions. *The Gerontologist*, 13, 282–8.
40. Pillemer, K.A. and Moore, D.W. (1989) Abuse of patients in nursing homes: findings from a staff survey. *The Gerontologist*, 29 (3), 314–20.
41. Straus, M.A. (1979) Measuring intra-family conflict and violence: the conflicts tactic (CT) scales. *Journal of Marriage and the Family*, 48, 465–79.
42. National Institute for Social Work. (1988) *Residential Care: A Positive Choice*. Report of the Independent Review of Residential Care, chaired by Gillian Wagner. HMSO, London.
43. Challis, L. and Bartlett, H. (1988) *Old and Ill: Private Nursing Homes for Elderly People*. Age Concern, London.
44. Gibbs, I. and Sinclair, I. (1992) Residential care for elderly people: the correlates of quality. *Ageing and Society*, 12 (4), 463–82.
45. Phillipson, C. and Walker, A. (1986) Conclusion: alternative forms of policy and practice. In *Ageing and Social Policy* (ed. Phillipson, C. and Walker, A.). Gower, Aldershot.

9

Research

During the 1980s the phenomenon of elder abuse was focused upon by researchers in the field of family violence. The 'discovery' of child abuse in the 1960s and domestic violence/spouse abuse in the 1970s led directly to the construction of elder abuse as a social problem [1]. This view combined with other emerging issues: the increasing numbers of elderly frail people at risk of abuse [2], the long-term effects of community care policies upon the family care of older people [3], and a greater interest in the sociology of old age [4]. This amalgamation of ideas and issues led directly to the need for research to clarify basic questions asked by sociologists [5], gerontologists [6], social policy analysts [7], psychologists [8] and geriatricians [9, 10].

In the US elder abuse became perceived and recognized as a discrete social problem. This gained it access to specific resource provision and government/legislative legitimacy. The status of elder abuse is very different in the UK and although 'discovered' in the UK the issue became the concern of only a few British professionals and did not succeed in attracting public or government attention. The issue was raised again in the 1980s [11] but although many health and social care workers were aware of cases of older people being the victims of family violence there was little research to substantiate claims that elder abuse affected a significant proportion of the elderly population.

In the US, however, the early research work, although relying on anecdotal evidence and small-scale studies, succeeded in capturing the attention of the relatively powerful American Public Welfare Association. Within the space of a few years the Senate Select Committee on Aging heard evidence from several sources citing numerous examples. The hearings, six in total, reported that more than one million, or 4%, of older Americans were physically, emotionally, or financially abused by their relatives [12].

This exercise led to a proliferation in research studies which in turn helped developments in policy. The research findings, however, were difficult to interpret, using different methodologies and having a 'definitional disarray'. At a policy level several American States began to pass mandatory reporting laws during the early 1980s, and now all States have them with the possibility of legislation at the federal level. Resources have been channelled into Adult Protective Services, which are State-funded agencies whose role is to investigate alleged cases of elder abuse. The recognition of elder abuse in the USA and Canada has therefore steadily grown with substantial resources directed towards research.

Research has been particularly influential in the process of the construction of elder abuse as a social problem, a process which has been modelled using Blumer's theory of the stages through which social problems must pass before they are fully recognized [1, 13]. Developing from the early US research has been a strong emphasis on the need for prevalence studies [14, 15]. There is a consensus among researchers in the USA that the highest priority is the undertaking of prevalence studies utilizing large-scale national representative samples [16]. These would combine the key features of increasing knowledge about the possible causes of abuse, determining the extent of the problem, and maintaining the impetus for political action.

This is in marked contrast to European research in elder abuse. There has been practically no systematic European initiatives in this area apart from the UK. The awareness of elder abuse by social and health care workers is therefore correspondingly low. The small number of UK publications are mainly limited to case studies or small projects [17–20, D. Jeffreys, 1990, unpublished report]. One important British study [10] is an attempt to measure the extent of abuse amongst a particular population of older people: disabled older persons in receipt of respite care. Fifty-one carers of older people who used a hospital-based resource for respite care were interviewed over a six-month period. Carers were asked whether they had ever felt like slapping, shoving, pushing, or hitting their elderly relatives. If the response was positive, carers were then asked if they had ever found themselves inflicting one of the four abusive behaviours on their elderly relatives, and twenty-three carers (45%) responded positively to this question. Abuse was defined in the study using an abbreviated version of the Conflict Tactics Scale, a research measurement tool developed in family violence studies in the USA (and discussed in detail later). However, it is not possible to generate any firm conclusions applicable to a wider population from this relatively small-scale study.

A further indication of elder abuse amongst a particular population of older people is provided by Levin *et al.* [21]. In a study of 150 older people living at home, suffering from confusion, and being cared for by relatives, two in three supporters sometimes or frequently lost their tempers with relatives. Furthermore, one-fifth of supporters had resorted at least once to hitting or shaking their elderly relative. It should also be noted that one-fifth of the confused elderly people had also recently hit out at their supporters, many of whom were themselves elderly. This fact introduces the complex notion of 'two-way' abuse, also found in a British study of community psychiatric support to confused elderly people [19].

Elsewhere in Europe, research concerning the prevalence of elder abuse is equally sparse. In Sweden a telephone survey of the general population to determine the extent to which respondents knew of violence committed against older persons produced a figure of 17% [22]. Although no comprehensive French studies have been undertaken there is clearly an awareness of elder abuse and envisaged research projects for the future [23]. It is generally acknowledged by practitioners and policy makers, therefore, that more needs to be known about the extent to which elder abuse can be said to be a social problem in Europe [22].

At the present time there is renewed interest amongst social and health care practitioners in elder abuse. Many local authorities are devising procedural guidelines and implementing training courses for staff [24]. There is a growing recognition that legislation to protect vulnerable elders is inadequate and the Law Commission is considering changes in cases where mental incapacitation may place older people at risk of abuse or exploitation [25]. A number of options have been put forward for consultation including the introduction of an Emergency

Assessment Order giving powers to intervene in serious urgent cases, and multidisciplinary sociolegal tribunals for complex cases. The Social Service Inspectorate has produced a report outlining the need for social service departments to develop training and procedures [20].

METHODOLOGICAL ISSUES

One of the first considerations for researchers of elder abuse is the question of how 'abuse' is to be defined and measured if attempts are to be made to quantify it. The problem of how to define abuse so that it can be meaningfully measured is not, however, unique to elder abuse research. Studies in child abuse and domestic violence have also been confronted with problems of definition. It is important, therefore, to consider how other family violence research has operationalized concepts to make possible their measurement and thus determine both prevalence and incidence.

Much of the research on family violence has focused upon the problem of child abuse. In the UK an oft-quoted source of information on child abuse is the number of reported cases known either to Social Services Departments or to the National Society for the Prevention of Cruelty to Children [26]. Both of these agencies are required to record basic information on suspected and actual child abuse in the form of Child Protection Registers. These registers can therefore provide a relatively accessible source of information on types of abuse together with local and national trends. There is also the advantage that some limited comparison of data is possible in so far as there are commonly held categories of physical abuse and neglect. The registers are likely, however, to provide a considerable underestimation of the extent of abuse, since they are a record of the number of reported cases only. Some studies have attempted to gain more accurate accounts by direct interviewing with families or individuals [27, 28]. Not surprisingly these studies have tended to report a greater prevalence of child abuse than the incidence figures of reported cases. Surveys in child abuse have been precise in their definition of abuse, often citing behaviours and their occurrence as the basis of measurement tools.

The most widely accepted measurement tool in family violence studies has been the Conflict Tactics Scale (CTS), developed by Straus [29]. This scale uses a set of behaviours by which families resolve conflicts. The fact that conflict is an inevitable part of human behaviour serves as the basis from which the scale is created. There are, of course, an infinite number of behaviours by which conflict is resolved. Straus, however, chooses three groups of behaviours which seem to be universally applicable: the use of reasoning and rational discussion, the use of verbal or non-verbal acts that 'symbolically hurt the other', and the use of physical force. These behaviours are graduated, with extreme coerciveness and behaviours that meet with high social disapproval appearing towards the end of the scale. Straus indicates that the CTS has been shown to have moderate to high reliability and that it can be used under a variety of conditions, including face-to-face interviews and postal questionnaires. Where the CTS has not been employed as an assessment tool, prevalence surveys into family violence have still included questions on direct behaviours, such as 'within the past year have you been in any situation in which violence has been used against you?' [30].

Previous research on elder abuse has therefore adopted one of two possible methodologies. The first approach can be seen in studies focused upon identified and reported cases, to compare characteristics such as age, class, levels of dependency, illness, and disability amongst other variables [31–33]. Nearly all of this research involves interviews with social and health care practitioners, and is firmly based upon the experience of early research in child abuse, particularly the theoretical models of the 'medicalization' of the problem. The second approach and, it is argued, the most powerful in terms of identifying prevalence and uncovering processes (and therefore possibly unknown variables) involves interviewing people directly about their experience of abuse. This can take the form either of direct interviews with victims and perpetrators, or randomly selected samples of older people from a general population in an attempt to determine prevalence or incidence.

To ask individuals whether they have recently been or are being abused is a request for intimate and deeply sensitive information. There are a variety of reasons, some practical, others psychological, why respondents may feel reluctant or unable to volunteer such information. Existing literature provides conflicting accounts concerning the ability of abused individuals to reveal, disclose, or share their experiences with researchers. In general, American research suggests that studies are possible which seek to determine the prevalence or incidence of abuse by asking respondents whether they have been abused [27, 33]. It also appears to be the case that abusers of older people are, given the right circumstances of a sympathetic and understanding researcher/interviewer relationship, able to talk about abusive behaviours inflicted on others. This appears to be particularly the case where there is a 'stressed caregiver' whose ability to acknowledge abuse is both cathartic and understandably linked to the possibility of greater support from the helping services. It is probable, therefore, that researchers who are themselves social and health care practitioners may have a better chance to access abusive situations, given that they may already be in some form of clinical or therapeutic contact with the individual.

RESEARCHING A SENSITIVE TOPIC

The abuse of an individual by a person or persons is an emotive and value-laden topic of enquiry. Where abuse has occurred the effect upon the victim and those who attempt to resolve it can be traumatic. Social and health care workers have found that there are considerable social sanctions and taboos in force against the abuse of family members, especially towards older persons. It can be extremely difficult for an abused older person and their family to acknowledge that abuse is taking place, and consequently workers in the social and health care field are faced with problems of recognition and disclosure. As in child abuse, those practitioners who work with abused older people are influenced in their interpretation of abuse by their value judgements, moral, social, and cultural codes, and personal experience [34]. The discovery of abuse can cause profound ethical dilemmas over what course of action to take. It is not surprising, therefore, that many health and social care workers find this area of work demanding and stressful.

It is clear that any research into abusive behaviours necessarily entails both a consideration of how the methodology itself may affect respondents, together with the responsibilities and obligations the researcher has when abuse is discovered or disclosed. In short the research on elder abuse therefore has certain characteristics that warrant special consideration. These features have been described by Lee and Renzetti as pertaining to 'sensitive' topics [35]:

> . . . a sensitive topic is one which potentially poses for those involved a substantial threat, the emergence of which renders problematic for the researcher and/or the researched the collection, holding and/or dissemination of research data.

Whilst it is possible for any research topic to pose some form of threat, Lee and Renzetti suggest that there are four areas where research is more likely to be threatening:

(a) Research which intrudes into the private sphere or intimate personal experience.
(b) Research concerned with deviance and social control.
(c) Research where there is an impingement on the vested interests of powerful persons.
(d) Research which touches upon sacred things to those being studied which they do not wish profaned.

Although some research topics may appear to contain *a priori* elements of these threats, Lee and Renzetti maintain that the sensitive character of research lies less with the specific topic than with the relationship between that topic and its social context. Sensitivity is therefore revealed during the research process as methodological, technical, ethical, political, and legal problems are encountered and negotiated.

In approaching the topic of elder abuse it is evident that the nature of the subject matter would potentially involve a substantial threat as defined by Lee and Renzetti. The US research on elder abuse is not informative in this area. In the early stages of the research design for a pilot study, although it was clearly recognized that the sensitivity of the research topic would influence and possibly constrain certain areas of enquiry, the full extent of its importance was not realized until the data collection was well under way [J. Ogg, unpublished dissertation]. Furthermore it became increasingly clear that the 'substantial threats' posed by the subject matter were indeed compounded, as Lee and Renzetti suggested, by the social context in which the research took place. In his pilot study Ogg indicates that access to respondents, gaining informed consent, confidentiality, the role of the researcher in the interview, and the dissemination of data were all highly influenced by the sensitivity of the research topic. These key areas need to be explored more closely.

ACCESS TO RESPONDENTS

Most research involves negotiations with 'gate-keepers' to obtain access to respondents. Consideration has to be given to the sensitive nature of the topic when deciding the best method for sampling. In practice, access to respondents is inextricably linked to sampling and gaining informed consent. In most community-based research early discussions with GPs, social workers, district nurses, and the voluntary sector usually reveal an initial willingness to provide potential respondents for study. It is clear, however, that potential conflicts of interest can arise between the research aims and those agencies providing a statutory or public service. If abuse is discovered during the research process, what obligations does the researcher have to pass on information to the agency who provided access to the respondent?

A further consideration is the possible effect of the sensitive questions upon the relationship between the respondent and the gate-keeper. Most gate-keepers can provide lists of potential respondents but are not usually aware of the threat to a change in their relationship with the respondent and the immediate family brought about by information disclosed. Sampling from lists that are not provided by a third party or gate-keeper can circumvent this problem, as can door-to-door surveys. However, it should be pointed out that the 'brief encounter' nature of the door-to-door survey can produce the opposite effect from that of the unintended intervention into the case management of a patient or service user – the potential threat posed to respondents by the sensitivity of the topic leaves them with little or no recourse to follow up the many issues which may be raised by talking about family violence.

GAINING INFORMED CONSENT

Whatever the research topic there is always the dilemma of how much information a potential respondent needs to be given in order to make an informed decision on whether to participate or not in the study [36]. The sensitivity of researching elder abuse compounds this essentially ethical problem. How much should respondents be told about the contents and nature of the Conflict Tactics Scale for example, containing direct questions of whether any family member has been violent towards the respondent, when having the aims of the research explained to them? There are strong arguments against a candid approach, since this runs the risk of potentially distressing the older person by the frankness of the explanation on the aims of family violence research. There are also the methodological problems of a resulting biased sample on the assumption that individuals who were or had recently been subjects of abuse would decline to take part.

Alternatively the objective of the research may be to identify cases and types of abuse, and to not make this clear to potential respondents could be construed as misleading or even deceitful. There is evidence to suggest that response rates to surveys on sensitive issues including alcohol consumption, drug use, sexual behaviour, and mental health are not significantly affected by informed consent procedures [36]. In the case of any hospital- or medical-based/initiated research, guidance (and indeed mandatory actions) are given by the local health authority Ethics Committee. Their usual view is that potential respondents should be clearly told about the content of questions contained in the research study.

Ethics Committees also place strong emphasis on the necessity of potential respondents to opt-in to any study as opposed to opting-out. The distinction between opting-in and opting-out is not always self-evident. Generally speaking, opting-in refers to the respondent, having been informed of the research, taking a proactive approach either in writing or verbally, to enter the study. The onus is therefore on the individual to contact the researcher to enter the study. With opting-out, the researcher starts from the premise that having informed potential respondents of the research aims it is not clear whether they wish to participate or not (unless the researcher is explicitly informed by an individual) until subsequent attempts are made to gain the potential respondent's participation. Ethics Committees usually require respondents to opt-in, thereby increasing the methodological problem of a biased sample, as it may be assumed that there are no incentives for respondents to opt-in to a study, and more importantly many good reasons why individuals should choose not to enter a sensitive study. Researchers with older people have generally found a greater willingness for them to participate in research than younger adults, posing a further ethical dilemma [37].

Should the readiness to partake in studies often shown by older people be regarded as an attribute or a methodological weakness open to exploitation?

CONFIDENTIALITY

It is an axiom of social research practice that confidentiality and anonymity should be maintained at all stages of the research process. For many research topics, upholding the confidentiality of information gained from interviews is relatively unproblematic. However, researching elder abuse poses some difficult ethical questions regarding confidentiality. What course of action should the researcher take when abuse is discovered during the research process and the respondent does not wish to accept the offer of any services to address the problems surrounding that abuse? An older woman may reveal during the course of an interview that her husband's violence towards her is increasing with the onset of some health problems. Should the researcher respect the woman's wish for confidentiality? If a subsequent tragedy were to occur and it became public knowledge that the researcher was aware of the abuse, would there be ensuing criticism? The fact that elder abuse tends to be associated with a degree of frailty and vulnerability compounds the dilemmas facing the researcher over whether to break the confidentiality of the information obtained during the interview. This is an issue often not resolved in research designs. In the specific study on hospital patients by Ogg [unpublished dissertation] it was decided that whilst maintaining the general principle of confidentiality, each case of abuse would be discussed with the consultant geriatrician who provided the name of the respondent. In the event of a most extreme case of abuse being located the clinician would take a decision as to whether to act to protect the older person, thus essentially breaking confidentiality.

THE ROLE OF THE RESEARCHER

Once a respondent has given consent to participate in research, consideration should be given to the location of the interview. Interviews may take place in a respondent's home but then there is always the possibility that other family members (spouses and adult children would be the most common) would be present. In such circumstances the interviewer would have to request that the interview with the respondent took place in private – not always an easy or even reasonable request to make. Interviews should always take place in comfortable and safe surroundings. The rigours of good interviewing skills are beyond the scope of this chapter but include patience, pacing, and punctuality on behalf of the interviewer.

DISSEMINATION OF DATA

The fact that a topic is sensitive should alert the researcher to the possible uses to which the data may be put on completion of the study. No research can be regarded as impartial and separate from the social and political framework within which it is undertaken. Although the anonymity of respondents is ensured it is not uncommon for many people, including those who decline to take part, to remain uncertain as to what purpose the findings would serve. The justification for socio-medical research is usually presented to respondents as alerting policy makers to the fact that such an occurrence (e.g. elder abuse) exists in a domestic setting. However, it should not be assumed that there is a positive link between research findings and policy developments.

The method of disseminating any data will necessarily have to take account of the audience to whom it is to be directed, e.g. media, social and health care professions, and academic institutions. The sensitivity of a topic increases the likelihood, particularly in relation to the media, of sensationalism.

US RESEARCH: THE BOSTON PREVALENCE STUDY OF ELDER ABUSE

Pillemer and Finkelhor [14] sampled 2020 people aged 65 years and over in a metropolitan area of Boston, Massachusetts. This

No matter how well a couple gets along, there are times when they disagree on major decisions, get annoyed about something the other person does, or just have spats or fights because they're in a bad mood or tired or for some other reason. They also use many different ways of trying to settle their differences. I'm going to read a list of some things that you and your (husband/partner) might have done when you had a dispute, and would first like you to tell me for each one how often you did it in the past year.

Hand Respondent Card A

	Q.78 Respondent – In Past Year								Q.79 Husband/Partner – In Past Year								Q.80 Ever Happened		
	Never	Once	Twice	3–5 Times	6–10 Times	11–20 Times	More than 20 Times	Don't Know	Never	Once	Twice	3–5 Times	6–10 Times	11–20 Times	More than 20 Times	Don't Know	Yes	No	Don't Know
a. Discussed the issue calmly	0	1	2	3	4	5	6	X	0	1	2	3	4	5	6	X	1	2	X
b. Got information to back up (your/his) side of things	0	1	2	3	4	5	6	X	0	1	2	3	4	5	6	X	1	2	X
c. Brought in or tried to bring in someone to help settle things	0	1	2	3	4	5	6	X	0	1	2	3	4	5	6	X	1	2	X
d. Insulted or swore at the other one	0	1	2	3	4	5	6	X	0	1	2	3	4	5	6	X	1	2	X
e. Sulked and/or refused to talk about it	0	1	2	3	4	5	6	X	0	1	2	3	4	5	6	X	1	2	X
f. Stomped out of the room or house (or yard)	0	1	2	3	4	5	6	X	0	1	2	3	4	5	6	X	1	2	X
g. Cried	0	1	2	3	4	5	6	X	0	1	2	3	4	5	6	X	1	2	X
h. Did or said something to spite the other one	0	1	2	3	4	5	6	X	0	1	2	3	4	5	6	X	1	2	X

Figure 9.1 The Conflict Tactics Scale.

		0	1	2	3	4	5	6	X		0	1	2	3	4	5	6	X
i.	Threatened to hit or throw something at the other one	0	1	2	3	4	5	6	X		0	1	2	3	4	5	6	X
j.	Threw or smashed or hit or kicked something	0	1	2	3	4	5	6	X		0	1	2	3	4	5	6	X
k.	Threw something at the other one	0	1	2	3	4	5	6	X		0	1	2	3	4	5	6	X
l.	Pushed, grabbed, or shoved the other one	0	1	2	3	4	5	6	X		0	1	2	3	4	5	6	X
m.	Slapped the other one	0	1	2	3	4	5	6	X		0	1	2	3	4	5	6	X
n.	Kicked, bit, or hit with a fist	0	1	2	3	4	5	6	X		0	1	2	3	4	5	6	X
o.	Hit or tried to hit with something	0	1	2	3	4	5	6	X		0	1	2	3	4	5	6	X
p.	Beat up the other one	0	1	2	3	4	5	6	X		0	1	2	3	4	5	6	X
q.	Threatened with a knife or gun	0	1	2	3	4	5	6	X		0	1	2	3	4	5	6	X
r.	Used a knife or gun	0	1	2	3	4	5	6	X		0	1	2	3	4	5	6	X
s.	Other (PROBE): _____	0	1	2	3	4	5	6	X		0	1	2	3	4	5	6	X

79. And what about your (husband/partner)? Tell me how often he (ITEM) in the past year. _____

For each item circled either 'Never' or 'Don't Know' for BOTH respondent and partner, ask:

80. Did you or your (husband/partner) ever (ITEM)? _____

Figure 9.1 continued.

random stratified sample was obtained by means of a published and publically accessible list of the residents of every household. Several interviewers were employed, using a structured questionnaire to ask a series of questions concerning the family life of older people. A considerable proportion of the interviews were conducted by telephone.

The interview schedule, in addition to common variables such as age, sex, class, education, and family composition, included two core elements which were concerned with abuse and neglect. Abuse was divided into two categories: physical abuse and psychological abuse. Each category was then operationalized using the following indicators: for physical abuse a modified form of the Conflict Tactics Scale (CTS) was used (Figure 9.1). This assessment tool was developed in family violence studies by Straus [29]. The scale uses a set of behaviours by which families resolve conflicts. The fact that conflict is an inevitable part of human behaviour serves as the basis from which the scale is created. There are, of course, an infinite number of behaviours by which conflict is resolved. However, Straus chooses three groups of behaviours which seem to be universally applicable: the use of reasoning and rational discussion, the use of verbal or non-verbal acts that 'symbolically hurt the other', and the use of physical force. These behaviours are graduated, with extreme coerciveness and behaviours that meet with high social disapproval appearing towards the end of the scale. Straus indicates that the CTS has been shown to have moderate to high reliability and that it can be used under a variety of conditions, including face-to-face interviews and postal questionnaires [29].

In the Boston elder abuse study, if the older respondent disclosed that any person in his or her family or close social network had been violent towards him or her at least once since becoming 65 years old, then they were placed in the physical abuse category. Psychological abuse was measured by the existence of repeated insults and threats, forming a category labelled as 'chronic verbal aggression'. If the respondent had been insulted, sworn at, or threatened more than 10 times in the preceding year, they were placed in the 'psychological abuse' category. The final category, 'neglect', was operationalized by the inclusion of 10 important activities of daily living, including the preparation of meals, housework, and personal

Table 9.1 Rates of elder abuse in Boston, USA

Type of abuse	Rate/1000	95% Confidence interval	Projected no. in Boston population
All types	32	25–39	8646–13 487
Physical violence	20	14–26	4841–8991
Neglect	4	1–7	346–2421
Chronic verbal aggression	11	7–15	2420–5187

care. If help was needed by the respondent in any of these areas and it had been withheld by a close family member more than 10 times in the preceding year (the respondent deeming this omission to be somewhat or very serious), he or she was then placed in the 'neglect' category. The results of the Boston elder abuse survey are shown in Table 9.1. In addition the Boston study reported that over half the perpetrators of abuse (58%) were spouses, thereby suggesting that domestic violence accounts for a substantial proportion of elder abuse.

A UK NATIONAL ABUSE STUDY

The failure of elder abuse to be recognized as a social problem in Britain can be attributed in part to a lack of research findings which would conclusively establish its existence. During 1992 Bennett and Ogg, of the Department of Health Care of the Elderly at the Royal London NHS Trust, were approached by an independent TV production company (Fulcrum Productions Ltd) who were interested in making a documentary on elder abuse. The company was reluctant, however, to produce the documentary in the absence of any figures to indicate that elder abuse is a social problem of the type indicated by the health and social care practitioners working in this field. The possibility of a small national research project on elder abuse to be carried out in a short period of time appeared to be the kind of work which the Omnibus section of the Office of Population Census Surveys (OPCS) would find feasible. The OPCS Omnibus Survey is a monthly survey undertaken for government departments and public bodies. The Omnibus field staff interview around 2000 adults aged 16 years or over in approximately 100 sites throughout the UK each month, thereby producing a representative random sample of the population. Response rates are in excess of 75% and usually around 80% [38]. In addition to data collected by the OPCS for their own use, the Omnibus survey offers the facility of purchasing a module to address a particular research question. The results of the survey contain a number of standard classificatory variables which the OPCS collect each month, including amongst others, sex, marital status, social class, and the responses to the specially designed module.

Contact was made with the relevant social survey officer within OPCS to discuss the feasibility of running a module on elder abuse. Initial discussions centred upon the context of the research question within social policy, as the Omnibus team was unfamiliar with the current debate on elder abuse. The Boston elder abuse methodology and the sensitive nature of the topic were also discussed. In addition the financing from Channel 4 to Fulcrum Productions Ltd allowed for only a small number of questions to be asked in the module (a maximum of 7 or 8). It was therefore important to consider whether any meaningful data could be obtained from a small number of questions concerning such a complex phenomenon as elder abuse.

The OPCS's reaction was favourable from the outset, although they conceded that this was a new area for them to research. There was therefore a degree of trepidation on their part regarding the effect of researching a sensitive topic upon interviewers and more importantly the general public. Researching a sensitive topic was not entirely new for the OPCS, as they had carried out an Omnibus survey on condom use. However, the design of the interview schedule did not proceed until the OPCS had consulted with both the Department of Health and the Home Office regarding any possible repercussions from this type of research. Although the details of these discussions are not known, it may be assumed that the possible political implications from the proposed survey were high on the agenda.

After several drafts a final questionnaire was produced for use in the Omnibus survey. The interviewer reads a short paragraph to respondents aged over 60 years to place the questions in context:

The questions are about problems and disagreements that can arise in families. However well people get on with their families and people who are close to them, arguments can arise and someone may do something to upset someone else. Thinking over the last few years, will you please look at these cards and tell me if anything of this sort has happened to you?

There followed three questions to the older respondent, one each in the area of verbal, physical, and financial abuse. The questions on verbal and physical abuse contain behaviours which formed part of the Conflict Tactics Scale. In addition, the respondent was asked whether they had been frightened by the verbal abuse. Because there was no scope for interviewers to record additional data such as the frequency or intensity of abuse, it was important to try and establish if the verbal abuse had a negative effect upon the respondent which placed the behaviour outside 'normal' family patterns.

Each of the three questions on verbal, physical, and financial abuse was followed by asking when this behaviour last occurred. This was important for two reasons. Firstly, unless some time-scale was placed on the behaviour's occurrence, it would be extremely difficult to determine if in fact the abuse had occurred in old age. Secondly, it was important to determine whether any patterns existed in the time-scales when the abuse had occurred. It may be argued that the most recent events are most likely to be those which the respondent recalls. However, in a sensitive topic such as abuse, recent experiences may be too emotionally painful for respondents to reveal to an interviewer. Allowing the respondent to distance themselves in time from an abusive behaviour by a family member may make it somewhat easier for them to disclose.

The second part of the questionnaire was directed towards all the respondents in the survey, i.e. including all adults over 16 years old. The field interviewer first checked whether the respondent was in regular contact with a person of pensionable age. An introductory paragraph was then read:

People in close contact with one another can sometimes be under a lot of stress for various reasons. Will you please look at this card and tell me if anything of this sort has ever happened to you over the last few years.

Two questions on the subject of verbal and physical abuse were then asked. These questions were designed to represent the reversal of the first two questions directed towards older people. With the small number of questions which the budget allowed, identifying carers became problematic. Being in regular contact was therefore designed to encompass all those people. Carers would be included in this group, although it was not possible to determine what proportion were carers or the nature of the caring task. Homer and Gilleard's study [10] had indicated that many carers were able to acknowledge abusive behaviours directed towards dependent elderly relatives. It was important therefore to determine whether this was the case where the respondent had no previous contact with the interviewer and therefore no clinical or therapeutic relationship.

In constructing an interview schedule with a limited number of questions it was necessary to keep the definitions of 'abuse' intentionally broad. The questions were based upon the items of behaviour which had been used in the Conflict Tactics Scale. However, there was no scope, because of the limited resources, to develop these indicators of abuse by asking questions relating to the frequency and severity of incidents and by whom the abuse was inflicted. Because the definitions were kept broad it was possible and indeed probable that results would contain behaviours which may not be 'abusive' in terms of their severity and intensity. Nevertheless, the wide definitions adopted would at the very least serve as an indicator of whether these sensitive questions could be asked in a large-scale survey.

The questionnaire was administered nationally in 100 different areas in May 1992. The number of interviews achieved was 2130.

The sampling frame was drawn from the Post Office's Postcode Address File of 'small users', which includes all household addresses. One hundred postal sectors were selected throughout Britain, following stratification by region, the proportion of households renting from local authorities, and the proportion in which the head of household is in socioeconomic groups 1–5 or 13 (i.e. a professional, employer, or manager). Only one adult per household was interviewed.

The OPCS employs a pool of interviewers trained to carry out surveys. Advance letters are sent to all addresses, giving a brief account of the survey. Interviewers call at all the selected addresses unless a refusal has been made beforehand in response to the advance letter. The OPCS's method of selecting respondents does not entail notification of the precise details and aims of the survey. Respondents were aware that they would be asked questions on a wide range of topics before giving consent to participate. However, they were not aware prior to the interview that questions on abusive behaviours would form part of the research. The problem of obtaining informed consent for a particularly sensitive research topic which causes many problems in other settings did not arise in the Omnibus survey. Respondents were of course free to choose not to answer any questions, but the probability of a high response was much greater having circumvented the opting in or opting out dilemmas of local ethics committees.

Because only one household member is interviewed, people in households containing few adults have a greater chance of selection than those in households with many adults. The OPCS therefore apply a weighting (weight A) to correct for the unequal probability of households containing different numbers of adults entering the sample. Responses are first weighted by the number of adults in the household to correct the proportions, and then adjusted to give a total sample size equal to the number of respondents actually interviewed [39]. The achieved sample is therefore subject to sampling errors arising from these weighting procedures, and these errors add to the observed variance of the sample. The resulting design effect would tend to increase the range of the confidence intervals, although previous Omnibus surveys have found this increase to be negligible.

The results from the elder abuse module are shown in Tables 9.2 and 9.3.

Of the 593 individuals aged 65 years and over, 32 (5%) reported having been verbally abused by a close family member or relative, nine (2%) reported physical abuse, and nine (2%) reported financial abuse. The fact that some older people are frightened by the verbal abuse of close family members raises several questions concerning the nature of the abuse and its possible causes. More women (7%) than men (4%) are verbally abused, although there is a slightly higher proportion of men who reported physical and financial abuse (3%) than women (1%). Of particular interest is whether the verbal abuse experi-

Table 9.2 Number of elderly people reporting abuse

Type of abuse	Total number (%)	Male (%)	Female (%)	Percentage reporting abuse within the last year
(a) Verbal	32 (5)	11 (4)	21 (7)	65
(b) Physical	9 (2)	7 (3)	2 (1)	53
(c) Financial	9 (2)	7 (3)	2 (1)	82
	$n = 593$	$n = 283$	$n = 310$	

Table 9.3 Reported numbers of abuses to elderly people by adults in regular contact with an elderly person

Type of abuse	Total number (%)	Male (%)	Female (%)
(a) Verbal	126 (9)	59 (9)	78 (11)
(b) Physical	12 (0.9)	6 (1)	6 (1)
	$n = 1366$	$n = 654$	$n = 712$

enced by 5% of the sample is associated with any aspect of the 'ageing' process, such as disability, poverty, or kinship relations. It is, of course, not possible to draw any firm conclusions from the limited data other than the fact that verbal abuse, as defined in the survey, is experienced by some older people. Equally, the small but significant number of older people who reported some form of physical abuse raises further questions regarding the nature of this abuse and by whom it was inflicted. Three per cent of males over 60 years reported physical abuse as compared to 1% of females. This finding could suggest that domestic violence may not be the primary cause of physical elder abuse, as was found in the Boston study [14]. As details of the 'abuser' are not known, it is difficult to speculate on the origins of this form of abuse. Financial abuse has always been an elusive concept to measure, with practically no systematic research to confirm its existence; it is, however, a form of abuse that is beginning to be recognized and recorded by social and health care practitioners, particularly as some older people have considerable material and financial assets [40].

The fact that over half the responses had occurred within the last year demonstrates perhaps that respondents are able to disclose in a research setting abusive behaviours which they have recently experienced. In this respect the use of a limited number of questions which do not probe too deeply into the intimate spheres of family life may be more productive than the detailed questionnaires used in the US studies. This result should provide some impetus and encouragement to further similar studies being undertaken.

Of 1366 adults aged over 16 years who have regular contact with someone of pensionable age, 126 (9%) acknowledged verbally abusing and 12 (0.9%) physically abusing them. (A question on financial abuse was not included because of budgetary limitations.) The number of adults who found themselves verbally abusing an older person (9%) is higher than the 5% of older adults who acknowledged verbal abuse by family members. This discrepancy may be due to disclosure problems by elderly people. The reported number of adults who said they had physically abused an older person (0.6%) is low, but comparable with the Canadian findings of 0.5% [15].

Although the results are statistically low, the benefits of a representative national survey are that the results can be used to estimate prevalence within the general population, as is shown in Table 9.4.

The numbers of abused elderly people in the general population were estimated by calculating 2 standard errors around the sample proportion (using the conventional standard error of a proportion formula), based on the age distribution figures of the 1981 census data for people aged 60 years and above. For

Table 9.4 Estimates of survey results for British population

Abuse reported by elderly people	Type of abuse	95% confidence intervals for British population (×1000)
	Verbal	561–1123
	Physical	94–505
	Financial	94–505
Abuse reported to elderly people by adults aged 16 years and above	Verbal	2411–3305
	Physical	134–402

verbal and physical abuse reported by adults to an elderly person with whom they were in regular contact, estimations in the general population were again calculated using the conventional standard error of a proportion of the total sample (i.e. 2130 respondents). The calculations were based on the Registrar General's population estimate for 1990 of people in Britain aged 16 years and over. As stated previously the design effect of the sample does not significantly increase the calculation of interval estimates.

It can be seen that when estimates are produced for the general population some indication can be given as to the extent of elder abuse in Britain. The estimates contain wide intervals because of the relatively small sample and statistically low numbers of reported abuse cases. The figures should therefore be treated with some caution and a much larger sample would need to be obtained to be more precise as to the extent of elder abuse in the general population.

Although the methodologies of American, Canadian and British studies differ in detail, some comparison of the findings in these three countries is possible, as is shown in Table 9.5.

All the studies show a statistically low prevalence rate of abuse. Where the American and Canadian data have used indicators of abuse to uncover frequency and intensity, the results are lower than the British survey, as for example with verbal abuse. However, the fact that the rate of elder abuse for all three countries is under 5% suggests that the difficulties of comparing data from different methodologies is not so pronounced as would have been expected. Given the problems

Table 9.5 Comparison of rates of elder abuse by country

Type of abuse	RATE (%)		
	USA	Canada	Britain
All types	3.2	—	—
Physical	2.0	0.5	2.0
Verbal	1.1	1.4	5.0
Neglect	0.4	0.4	—
Financial/material	—	2.5	2.0

of obtaining accurate data, it may be that the similarity of results between studies is of greater relevance than the difference method. Any future development of elder abuse prevalence methodology will therefore need to consider carefully to what degree they are likely to achieve more precision, given that present research shows rates of under 5%. Further analysis of the results is available [J. Ogg, unpublished dissertation].

CONCLUSION

Ogg and Bennett's research on elder abuse was based on the assumption that it is important to determine to what extent elder abuse is a social problem in Britain [41]. In the absence of any recording or monitoring systems of elder abuse cases by agencies, it was argued that prevalence studies similar to those undertaken in the USA and Canada needed to be tried and tested. The piloting of an American elder abuse methodology raised several methodological and ethical problems of researching a sensitive topic [J. Ogg, unpublished dissertation]. A national survey with limited questions was undertaken which closely followed the American definitions of abuse. The survey does show, using broad definitions of abuse, that forms of abusive behaviours exist in the domestic setting. The fact that there were positive responses at all alerts us to the fact that some older people are victims of abuse. Whereas previously the absence of any random sample surveys of elder abuse allowed sceptics to point to a few cases amongst the most high-risk groups of older people, the undertaking of a national survey demonstrates that older people can be subjected to varying degrees and forms of abuse by family members and close relatives. The survey obviously raises more questions than it provides answers, yet clearly the results show that more knowledge is needed regarding the types and forms of abuse which have been located.

In so far as the theoretical issues raised have been addressed by the national elder abuse study, it is clear that little has been added to the knowledge of the causes of elder abuse. The results showed no significant association between structural factors and abuse but this is primarily due to the difficulties of comparing variables when the results are statistically low. At the same time there are no obvious indicators that a particular feature is associated with elder abuse. This should lead us to be more cautious of the portrait of the typical victim as being a white disabled woman aged over 75 which has been based primarily upon the American data.

The pilot study of the American methodology demonstrated the substantial ethical dilemmas which are involved in researching elder abuse, dilemmas which appear absent or ignored in the American studies [J. Ogg, unpublished dissertation]. The success of the Omnibus elder abuse survey, in so far as it produced any results at all, may be in part due to the fact that it was able to avoid the complex issues of gaining informed consent to participate in studying a sensitive research topic. It is difficult to conceive in the present climate how further prevalence studies, exclusively confined to elder abuse, would receive the necessary approval from Ethics Committees or their counterparts. This limits prevalence studies to random sample surveys based on the Electoral Register or any other sources whereby it may be possible to identify where older people live – a resource-intensive method of data collection, particularly when a low prevalence rate is anticipated. In addition, the piloting of the American methodology which was undertaken at the Royal London NHS Trust [J. Ogg, unpublished dissertation] suggests that in-depth interviews on elder abuse using community surveys may not be appropriate for the British population on both methodological and ethical grounds. If there are to be any further attempts at prevalence studies, they will have to address these issues seriously and perhaps consider alternative methodologies.

There are two possible alternative methodologies in research on elder abuse. Anecdotal evidence of elder abuse continues to suggest that a significant proportion of abused older people are already in receipt of some form of service provision. Rather than ask the question: 'How much elder abuse is there?', it is perhaps more appropriate to look at the characteristics of those abused older people and their family situations as they are known to the social and health care services. This means that comprehensive recording mechanisms must be developed for those cases that are already known to those services supporting older people and their carers. The second possibility for further research is to focus upon those older people who are vulnerable, by virtue of disability, poverty, or poor housing to name a few factors, to abuse and exploitation. It may be that the concept of vulnerability is of equal importance to that of abuse and that ultimately age itself is incidental to whether an individual is abused. Research that focuses upon vulnerability should therefore select predefined groups of vulnerable older people as the basis for their sample. This would include older people from the black and ethnic minority communities, particularly those living in areas of high social deprivation, where a combination of factors gives rise to vulnerability. Both of these research possibilities would need to incorporate a degree of qualitative analysis in order to address more closely the theoretical issues.

The research field in elder abuse is currently wide open. There is a desperate need for information on causation, intervention plans, education protocols, disclosure techniques, carer/ abuser characteristics, victim characteristics, the role of monitoring, legislation and the mentally frail, etc. In addition the umbrella concept of elder abuse covers the issue of institutional abuse. This too has numerous ethical and moral dilemmas, but good-quality research in this area is long overdue. Many dedicated health care professionals are working and researching in elder abuse but do not know of similar work being done elsewhere or of recent research findings. A charity, *Action on Elder Abuse*, was launched in 1993. It consists of interested professionals dedicated to the research and education process. It is being generously nurtured by Age Concern England and produces a newsletter to keep members abreast of the latest publications and research. Its mission statement is:

> To prevent elder abuse by promoting changes in policy and practice through raising awareness, education, research and the dissemination of information.

The national elder abuse prevalence study is but one aspect of several dimensions of elder abuse. Further research must focus clearly upon the circumstances under which different forms of abuse arise and in what settings. Although this particular piece of research confined itself to the abuse of older people in the domestic setting, we must not lose sight of the fact that the problem of elder abuse is a global and pervasive one. Elder abuse takes place in institutions, including residential homes and hospitals. Cases of financial abuse by staff employed as support workers by local authorities are known in practically every Social Services Department. Violence against older people by staff is not unknown. Crime against vulnerable older people, particularly fraud and burglary of older single women, continues to account for a substantial proportion of all crimes. Elder abuse, when viewed from all these perspectives, can be seen to have no single cause, but must be the result of the structural features of society which marginalize older people, of which ageism is the most pervasive. It is to be hoped that the evidence of the existence of elder abuse by researchers will contribute to a radical change in the perception of old age, a change that will allow later life to be enjoyed free from all forms of abuse.

REFERENCES

1. Leroux, T.G. and Petrunik, M. (1990) The construction of elder abuse as a social problem: a Canadian perspective. *The International Journal of Health Services*, 20 (4), 651–63.
2. Stevenson, O. (1989) *Age and Vulnerability*. Edward Arnold, London.
3. Pritchard, J. (1992) *The Abuse of Elderly People*. Jessica Kingsley, London.
4. Arber, S. and Ginn, J. (1990) The meaning of informal care: gender and the contribution of elderly people. *Ageing and Society*, 10, 429–54.
5. Steinmetz, S.K. (1990) Elder abuse: myth and reality. In *Family Relationships In Later Life* (ed. Brubaker, T.H.). 75–88.
6. Kosberg, J.I. (1988) Preventing elder abuse: identification of high risk factors prior to placement decisions. *The Gerontologist*, 28 (1), 43–50.
7. Horkham, E.M. (1990) *Study Group on Violence Against Older People.* Council of Europe, Brussels.
8. Browne, K.D. (1989) Family violence: spouse and elder abuse. In *Clinical Approaches to Violence* (ed. Howells, K. and Hollin, C.R.). Wiley, Chichester.
9. Bennett, G.C.J. (1990) Action on elder abuse in the 1990's: new definitions will help. *Geriatric Medicine*, 20 (4), 53–4.
10. Homer, A.C. and Gilleard, C. (1990) Abuse of elderly people by their carers. *British Medical Journal*, 301, 1359–62.
11. Eastman, M. (1984) *Old Age Abuse*. Age Concern, England.
12. US Congress House Committee on Aging (1981) *Elder Abuse: The Hidden Problem* (Comm. Pub. No. 96–220). US Printing Office, Washington DC.
13. Blumer, H. (1971) Social problems as collective behaviour. *Social Problems*, 18 (3), 298–306.

14. Pillemer, K. and Finkelhor, D. (1988) The prevalence of elder abuse: a random sample survey. *The Gerontologist*, 28 (1), 51–7.
15. Podnieks, E. (1989) *National Survey on the Abuse of the Elderly in Canada*. Ryerson Polytechnical Institute, Ottawa.
16. Stein, K.F. (1991) A national agenda for elder abuse and neglect research. *Journal of Elder Abuse and Neglect*, 3 (3), 91–108.
17. Eastman, M. (1982) Granny battering, a hidden problem. *Community Care*, 413, 27.
18. Pritchard, J. (1989) Confronting the taboo of the abuse of elderly people. *Social Work Today*, 21 (6), 12–13.
19. Wilson, G. (1991) Elder abuse – a hidden horror. *Critical Public Health*, 2, 32–8.
20. Social Services Inspectorate (1992) *Confronting Elder Abuse*. HMSO, London.
21. Levin, E., Sinclair, I. and Gorbach, P. (1989) *Families, Services and Confusion in Old Age*. National Institute for Social Work Research Unit, Aldershot, Avebury.
22. Violence against elderly people. (1992) A report prepared by the study group on violence against elderly people. Council of Europe, Brussels.
23. Hugonot, R. (1990) Violences Contre les Vieux, Eres, Toulouse.
24. Wright, M. and Ogg, J. (1992) Challenging stereotypes. *Community Care*, 947, 16–17.
25. Law Commission Report (1991) HMSO, London.
26. Taylor, S. (1989) How prevalent is it? In *Child Abuse and Neglect* (ed. Rogers, S.W., Hevey, D. and Ash, E.). Open University Press, London.
27. Straus, M.A. *et al.* (1981) *Behind Closed Doors*. Anchor Doubleday, New York.
28. Baker, A. and Duncan, S. (1986) Prevalence of child sexual abuse in Great Britain. *Child Abuse and Neglect*, 9, 457–69.
29. Straus, M.A. (1979) Measuring intra-family conflict and violence: the conflict tactics (CT) scales. *Journal of Marriage and the Family*, 41, 75–88.
30. Hanmer, J. and Saunders, S. (1984) *Well Founded Fear: A Community Study of Violence To Women*. Hutchinson, London.
31. Block, R. and Sinnott, J.D. (1979) Methodology and results. In *The Battered Elder Syndrome: an Exploratory Study* (ed. Block, M.R. and Sinnott, J.D.). Center on Aging, University of Maryland, College Park, MD.
32. Lau, E. and Kosberg, J.I. (1979) Abuse of the elderly by informal care givers. *Aging*, 2, 10–15.
33. Pillemer, K. (1986) Risk factors in elder abuse: results from a case-control study. In *Elder Abuse: Conflict in the Family* (ed. Pillemer, K. and Wolf, R.S.). Auburn House, Dover, MA.
34. Department of Health (1988) *Protecting Children: A Guide for Social Workers Undertaking a Comprehensive Assessment*. HMSO, London.
35. Lee, R. and Renzetti, C.M. (1990) The problems of researching sensitive topics. *Am. Behav. Sci.*, 33 (5), 510–28.

36. Bulmer, M. (ed.) (1979) *Censuses, Surveys and Privacy*. Macmillan, London.
37. Denham, M. (1984) The ethics of research in the elderly. *Age and Ageing*, 13, 321–7.
38. Office of Population Census Surveys (OPCS) (1992) Omnibus – details of the survey. OPCS, London.
39. Eliot, D. (1990) The use of the effective sample size as an aid in designing weighted samples. *Survey Methodology Bulletin*. Jan.
40. Fisk, J. (1991) Abuse of the Elderly. In *Psychiatry in the Elderly* (ed. Jacoby, R. and Oppenheimer, C.). Oxford University Press, Oxford.
41. Ogg, J. and Bennett, G.C.J. (1992) Elder abuse in Britain. *British Medical Journal*, 305, 998–9.

Index